RICHARD HUGHES
PLAYS

PLAYS

THE SISTERS' TRAGEDY
A COMEDY OF GOOD AND EVIL
THE MAN BORN TO BE HANGED
DANGER

RICHARD HUGHES

1966

CHATTO AND WINDUS

LONDON

Published by
Chatto & Windus Ltd.
42 William IV Street
London W.C.2

*

Clarke, Irwin & Co. Ltd.
Toronto

The Performing Rights of these plays are
fully protected, and permission to perform
them, whether by Amateurs or Professionals,
must be obtained in advance from the
author's Sole Agent, Marjory Vosper,
53a Shaftesbury Avenue, London W.1
from whom all particulars can be obtained.

First published 1924
First issued in the Phoenix Library 1928
This edition 1966

CONTENTS

THE SISTERS' TRAGEDY   p7

A COMEDY OF GOOD & EVIL   45

THE MAN BORN TO BE HANGED   149

DANGER   175

THE
SISTERS' TRAGEDY

NOTE

The Sisters' Tragedy was first performed privately at the house of Mr. John Masefield on January 24th, 1922.

The first public production opened in London at the Little Theatre on May 31st, 1922.

*

The Producer is asked to remember that though it was played in the *London Grand Guignol*, this is not essentially a Grand Guignol play, and should not be acted in the Grand Guignol manner; and that unless it is well acted it will be a complete failure. The part of Lowrie, especially, should be taken with great restraint. Each part has its own climax—Philippa, her lament for Owen; Charlotte, her single cry of "John!" at the very end; and Lowrie, her last speech. They should keep at least half their power in reserve for these climaxes.

CHARACTERS

THEY are all rather slovenly in appearance, suggesting a family possibly of county origin but for at least a generation impoverished and isolated and uneducated.

PHILIPPA is about twenty-eight, plain, with a rather grim mouth. She is elaborately but untidily and unfashionably dressed, in a way out of keeping with a country life.

OWEN is about twenty-four, tall and very thin, with the vacant, peevish air of a blind deaf-mute. The only sound he makes is a sort of throaty chuckle (referred to as "Owen's noise") by which he attracts attention to his wants, which he explains in dumbshow. His jaw drops rather.

CHARLOTTE is nineteen: a pretty, fair (but rather hard and characterless) face: she would look very pretty if properly dressed and taught how to walk and hold herself. When she enters, she is wearing an old pair of army riding-breeches and a torn silk evening jumper: her hair wildish.

LOWRIE is about thirteen, and very small and slight. She is superficially like CHARLOTTE, but not so pretty, and far more passionate and sensitive. All are bitten with the prevalent

4

Welsh piety of the neighbourhood; but in LOWRIE only does her imaginative power and curious trend of logic render this dangerous.

JOHN, who is by way of being CHARLOTTE'S fiancé, is quite obviously of a lower social class than the sisters, though they do not appear to see it; which completes the general air of running to seed. This vulgarity only becomes quite patent under the stress of emotion at the end of the play. In the first scene with LOWRIE his manner is a little bewildered, but good-natured; and he seems quite fond of her. One's first impression from their manner is that he is more in love with CHARLOTTE than she with him.

SCENE

THE hall in the sisters' house (an early-Victorian mansion in the Welsh hills), now used as a living-room. There is a front door up R., with a window to the left of it; a fire L., with an arm-chair facing the audience and another below it; and a door above it; a table littered with work-things, etc., centre. The walls are panelled, and there are dingy oil portraits, some of them torn: mostly crooked. The fur hearth-rug is moulted: a general air of past prosperity run to seed, untidiness, things put to their wrong uses. Decoration, such as it is, Victorian.

TIME

AUTUMN, early afternoon.

THE
SISTERS' TRAGEDY

PHILIPPA *discovered at window, looking out, one arm in a half-darned stocking.*

PHILIPPA. Kill it, Chattie, kill it!

CHARLOTTE [*without; exasperated*]. I can't.

PHILIPPA. Put it out of its pain at once, for heaven's sake.

CHARLOTTE [*without*]. I can't do it: you come.

PHILIPPA. Pull yourself together, Charlotte; hit it behind the ears with your shoe. Oh, be quick, it's screaming. [*Sound of a blow; steps heard running.*]

LOWRIE [*off*]. Oh, you brute, Chattie, what are you doing?

CHARLOTTE [*off*]. I've missed it.

LOWRIE [*off*]. Stop! stop! It might live! [*Another blow.*] O—oh, beast!

CHARLOTTE [*off*]. It's dead now, poor little thing. [*Enter* CHARLOTTE *by door up, dressed as above, hot but pale. She fits her shoe on in the doorway.*] It's dead now. It's a beastly business. I wish I hadn't been there and had to do it, it would have died anyhow in time. Somehow I couldn't hit straight, like in a dream. Silly of me. Cats are brutes.

PHILIPPA [*sitting down*]. I thought you were never going to finish.

CHARLOTTE. It must have been the little Joneses' rabbit got loose: Ginger could never have caught a wild one. I wish they'd look after it better, instead of letting it run about the garden and treating it like a pet. Poor little Anne, though.

PHILIPPA. It will be a lesson to her not to get so fond of brute animals. It isn't right.

CHARLOTTE. Well, *you* can tell her so. I've had enough of the whole business: she'll cry.— Lowrie has gone silly over it too: look at her.

[*Enter* LOWRIE *by door up, with something in her arms. Her head is bent forward, so that her long, loose hair covers her face. She moves quickly.*]

PHILIPPA. Don't bring it in the house, Lowrie. It must be buried.

LOWRIE [*to* PHILIPPA]. You brute, you told her to do it! Look at the blood in its eyes! [*To* CHARLOTTE:] Oh, you beast, Chattie, you murderer! You brute, though you are my sister, you——[*She bursts into tears and rushes as if to hit her.*]

PHILIPPA [*in a harsh voice*]. Lowrie!

[LOWRIE *stops dead.*]

PHILIPPA. Put that rabbit down! [LOWRIE *does so.*]

You dare hit your sister! What do you mean by behaving like this!

LOWRIE. She killed it.

PHILIPPA. She killed it to put it out of pain.

LOWRIE. Killing's murder.

PHILIPPA. You little fool, would you have let it go on screaming in agony?

LOWRIE. We might have nursed it.

CHARLOTTE [huffily]. Its back was broken.

LOWRIE. Do you mean it can ever be right to kill?

PHILIPPA. Of course it's right to put a thing out of its pain, you little idiot, when living is only a burden to it.

LOWRIE [nervously]. I don't know. Perhaps I'm silly. I thought there wasn't any arguing about killing: I thought it was just *wrong*. But are you sure it's right?—The Commandments, I mean . . .

PHILIPPA. Of course it's right, when it's done from high motives. You don't think John was wrong to shoot Germans, do you?

LOWRIE. No, of course, but Germans are different: this was a rabbit. Besides, it was his duty to do it.

CHARLOTTE. Well, you don't think I killed the little thing for pleasure, do you? Did I look as if I enjoyed it? I wish you'd be a bit more considerate of my feelings: I didn't want to do

it, and then you make it all the worse for
me by going on like this.

LOWRIE [*turning to her, with change of expression*].
Oh, Chattie, I'm so sorry. I'm a beast. I didn't
think. Do forgive me. I didn't see it like that,
and I've been a brute to you. I must think
about it all.

PHILIPPA. Very well, then; now you've said you're
sorry for your selfishness, you had better go
away to your room till you feel better.

[*Exit* LOWRIE. CHARLOTTE *picks up the
rabbit carelessly and strokes its fur; she sits
down.*]

CHARLOTTE. Thank goodness that's over.

PHILIPPA. I don't think we shall have any more
trouble from her. She has these naughty
tempers, but once she has said she's sorry,
she calms down.

CHARLOTTE. She's got a logical sort of mind, you
know: once she sees a point, like that, she
goes on ruminating on it for days.

PHILIPPA. She has no need to! She has far too
many ideas of her own about right and wrong
for her age, that child. She ought to be content
to do what she's told, instead of always reason-
ing about it.

CHARLOTTE. Oh, well, I think we're through with
this storm.

PHILIPPA. I'm not sure. You can never be quite sure with her. But I expect we are. It's a pity she was by; but she has got to meet that sort of thing some time.

CHARLOTTE. Shall we get John to skin it? If he killed another too, it would make a pair of slippers.

PHILIPPA. Oh, Charlotte, *could* you!

CHARLOTTE. Why not? You're as bad as Lowrie.

PHILIPPA. It doesn't seem right to make any *use* of a thing you have killed.

CHARLOTTE. I don't see it.

PHILIPPA. Well, let's talk about something more cheerful.

CHARLOTTE. What?

PHILIPPA. John.

CHARLOTTE [*in a lustreless voice*]. If you like.

PHILIPPA. When are you going to marry him?

CHARLOTTE. I don't know. Never.

PHILIPPA. You're a goose.

CHARLOTTE [*exasperated*]. Phil, how can I? How am I ever going to get away from this place?

PHILIPPA [*coldly*]. I say you are a goose. I am enough to look after Owen.

CHARLOTTE. How could I marry John and leave you to look after him all your life? People would jolly soon make my life a misery for me, for neglecting my duty. I know them!

PHILIPPA. Nonsense! You could go and live somewhere else.

CHARLOTTE. And what about you, anyway? Why should your life be sacrificed to him?

PHILIPPA. It's the Lord's will.

CHARLOTTE. You haven't spent a night away from the house for three years.

PHILIPPA. Why should I? I've got used to it. I—I should feel funny without dear old Owen. Anyhow, *I* don't want to get married.

CHARLOTTE. Have you never wanted to?

PHILIPPA [*pause*]. No [*meaning* "yes"].

CHARLOTTE. I suppose it's all right for you, then, if you're built that way. Self-sacrifice, I mean. But I'm not. I intend to get away some time.

PHILIPPA. Then go at once! Why not?

CHARLOTTE [*fiercely*]. Haven't I already told you I can't?

PHILIPPA. Don't worry about me! I am only doing what is right. I shall never regret it; not in this world, and I shall have my reward in the next. I intend to devote my whole life to Owen, and so make an offering acceptable unto the Lord.

CHARLOTTE. I see: you would prefer to be martyred comfortably at home, than have it done in some unhealthy jungle. It's not a bad idea.

PHILIPPA. Chattie! How can you! You forget one
must not think of oneself in these matters,
but of the object. It is Owen I am thinking of;
my duty lies at home; surely I may thank God
for that small mercy without thereby for-
feiting the full reward? It is wicked of you to
put it like that, it's unkind, when all I am
trying to do is to free you from your duty.

CHARLOTTE. It's not my duty you're trying to free
me from, it's my conscience.

PHILIPPA. Is it your conscience is troubling you?
Or what people will say, and perhaps the
heavenly consequences?

CHARLOTTE. Oh, shut up, Phil, you beast! Aren't
I refusing to go? What more do you want?
Besides, Owen may be taken away, and then
I *can* marry, and your old conscience can take
you to Somaliland or anywhere else horrid.

PHILIPPA. If you *like* to keep John waiting till
you're sixty, of course——

   [*Enter* LOWRIE *by door L. The sisters do
   not notice her, but she must never let the
   audience forget her presence during the scene,
   to which she pays a sort of abstracted attention.
   She picks up a book, but does not read it
   attentively.*]

CHARLOTTE [*suddenly*]. Phil, it's a shame! I almost
hate Owen when I see how he is wearing you out!

PHILIPPA. You mustn't talk like that, Chattie; you don't know how you hurt me. You never knew Owen like I did, before it happened. He was only seven. I shall always love him.

CHARLOTTE. All the same, it's a shame about all of us. Why should you and I and John have our lives spoilt for the sake of Owen, whose life really isn't worth living? Besides, it must be almost more awful for him than if he had been *born* blind and deaf, to lose them like that suddenly when he was seven years old, just through catching measles, and then to forget, actually to *forget* how to speak, too!— Phil, it makes me go cold to say it, but can God be just and merciful when He does things like that?

PHILIPPA. We are told that suffering is sent to chasten us.

CHARLOTTE. Told! Oh, yes, we're *told* often enough.

PHILIPPA. Oh, do stop! You're making it harder for me to bear, and God knows it is hard enough already. But there's no need if that's how you feel: haven't I always told you you are free to go away at any time? You won't do any good to yourself or anyone else by staying on in that frame of mind.

CHARLOTTE. And you?

PHILIPPA. I can bear it. It is what I am *for*.

CHARLOTTE. I can't go! I know you'll say it's wicked, but I almost pray that Owen may die. What's life to him, anyway? He isn't really alive, and he's killing you. Surely even in God's eyes your life is worth more than his.

PHILIPPA. Don't talk like that!

CHARLOTTE. I can't help *thinking* like that.

PHILIPPA. It's wicked; what good does it do, anyhow? Who are you to try and alter God's will? Besides, He may already have decided to take Owen to Him in His own way, by His own instrument unknown and even unguessed at by us. We know that He has never forgotten. Promise me you won't pray it.

CHARLOTTE. I can't promise.

PHILIPPA. You must, or I'll be miserable.

CHARLOTTE. Very well, then: but I'll still *think* it.

PHILIPPA. Where is he now, do you know?

CHARLOTTE. No, but I suppose he will be along presently.

[LOWRIE *gets up, and walks down the stage, carrying the book.* PHILIPPA'S *and* CHARLOTTE'S *manner changes immediately.*]

PHILIPPA. Reading?

LOWRIE [*wandering about aimlessly*]. Mm.

PHILIPPA. What?

LOWRIE. A tale. It was very silly.

PHILIPPA. Why don't you read better books, then?

LOWRIE. Because I don't like better books. It was about Mr. Badger. It's a story, at any rate. Have animals got Christian souls?

PHILIPPA. Why?

LOWRIE. I wondered. About that rabbit too: would he go to heaven?

PHILIPPA. No, he wouldn't go anywhere: he'd just die. But being nothing would be better for him than lingering on.

LOWRIE. It's better for Christians to go to heaven, anyhow, isn't it? I mean, however happy they are here, they'll be happier there, won't they? When old Mrs. Rhys died of the rheumatics, you said it was a merciful release. You told Ellen what a beautiful place her Grannie had gone to, didn't you, Phil? It's never just dying into blackness for a Christian, is it?

PHILIPPA. What are you asking such questions for?

LOWRIE. Is everyone who was christened Christian?

PHILIPPA. Why, yes.

LOWRIE. You're quite sure about all this?

PHILIPPA [sharply]. Quite.

LOWRIE. I suppose you're right. You must be.

[PHILIPPA catches CHARLOTTE's eye.]

CHARLOTTE. Lowrie, did you feed the bird to-day?

LOWRIE. No.

CHARLOTTE. Yesterday?

LOWRIE. I don't remember.

CHARLOTTE. Why can't you attend to your ordinary daily duties, instead of worrying about things like this which don't concern you? You'd better go and see whether *he*'s alive still, instead of arguing about people dying. [*Exit* LOWRIE *by door L.*] What a little devil she is for questioning! What is she getting at?

PHILIPPA. I don't know: there's obviously something running in her head. The worst of her is that whenever she gets into her head that something is right, she does it. It wouldn't matter otherwise.

CHARLOTTE. Do you think *she*'s going to pray for Owen to die?

PHILIPPA. I shouldn't think so; but you never can tell. I'll have to talk to her some time. Do you remember the time when she wouldn't eat meat, on her conscience? Why must she always be putting her twos to her twos, instead of leaving them quietly apart as the good God has put them? It's a bad habit, and makes me very worried about her sometimes.—Is John coming up to-day?

CHARLOTTE. I believe so: he's supposed to be going riding with me this afternoon. He ought to be here by now: I had forgotten.

PHILIPPA. *Forgotten!*

CHARLOTTE. Why not?

PHILIPPA. Oh.—Aren't you going to change that jumper?

CHARLOTTE. No. Why should I?

PHILIPPA. John, I mean.

CHARLOTTE. Oh, *he* won't mind.

[*Re-enter* LOWRIE.]

Is he still alive?

LOWRIE [*jumping*]. Who? Why?

CHARLOTTE. The bird.

LOWRIE. The bird? Oh, yes, I had fed him after all, and forgotten.

PHILIPPA [*to* CHARLOTTE]. I'd change it if I were you.

CHARLOTTE. Why? What does it matter?

[*There is a sound of hoofs off, and a voice calling* "Chattie."]

PHILIPPA. Hallo! Come right in.

[*Enter* JOHN.]

CHARLOTTE. All right, I'm coming.

PHILIPPA [*aside*]. Well, at any rate let me sew it up.

[*Exeunt together* PHILIPPA *and* CHARLOTTE *L.*]

JOHN [*warming his hands*]. Well, Lowrie, how's life?

LOWRIE. If you were driving a trap, John, and the wheel rolled over something small in the

road, and hurt it desperately but not so as
quite to kill it, what would you do?

JOHN. I'm tender-hearted, kid; unless I was in a
hurry I'd give it a belt with the whip-handle,
or perhaps a stone, to put it out of its pain.

LOWRIE. You're sure that's right?

JOHN. Why, of course.

LOWRIE. And yet animals don't have an after-
life, do they? It's really much more killing to
kill an animal than to kill a person?

JOHN. What do you mean?

LOWRIE. I don't know.—John, are you going to
marry Chattie?

JOHN [*sharply*]. Who said?

LOWRIE. But why shouldn't you?

JOHN [*slowly*]. I'm not saying I shouldn't.

LOWRIE. Then why don't you? Is it because of
Owen?

JOHN. Why?

LOWRIE. I wish he was dead.

JOHN. You mustn't say that, Lowrie, it's wicked.

LOWRIE. Don't *you*?

JOHN. I wouldn't *say* so.

LOWRIE. I can't see the difference. It's no great
joy to him being alive, and if he was dead he
would be in heaven, and you and Chattie
could get married. What's wrong in that?
He'd have ears and eyes in heaven.

JOHN. I'm not saying it wouldn't be better for *him*.

LOWRIE. Who wouldn't it be better for, then? What's Owen *for*?

JOHN. Well, he makes Phil able to live a life of self-sacrifice, and that's the best life a Christian *can* lead.

LOWRIE. Self-sacrifice is what's right?

JOHN. Of course it is. It makes people holy.

LOWRIE. Then you mean that really he is being sacrificed to her, not her to him? It's all very muddly.

[OWEN'S *noise heard off L., then fingers feeling on the door.* LOWRIE *runs to it, opens it, takes his arm, and leads him down to the chair by the fire facing the audience. This to be done slowly and emphatically. She comes back to* JOHN.]

LOWRIE [*to* JOHN]. Let him feel your sleeve [*does so*]. He likes to know who's here. Jack, you must make her marry you soon, and put Owen into a hospital somewhere. It's all very well to say suffering makes people holy: it isn't with her and Phil, it's making them ill-tempered; that's what it does with most people, it makes them cross and ill-tempered, and perhaps she won't go to heaven in the end at all, she's so snappy sometimes. Oh, John, I do love them. I'd do anything to make them happy, but I'll never be any use to anyone; but if only Owen would die, you could marry Chattie, and if Phil has a rest, she'd get quite young again.

[OWEN'S *noise, and he puts two fingers to his lips, sucking.* LOWRIE *lights a cigarette and gives it to him.*]

LOWRIE. When I was older I would offer to look after Owen myself, because I really love him too, only I know Phil would never let me, so that would be no good. I'd give my life not to see Phil unhappy like this: I'd let God send my soul to hell for her sake; that's sacrifice, isn't it?

JOHN. Lowrie, you're blaspheming! You're a good girl, but there's no need for that: you stick to doing all your little everyday duties, and try and save Phil all the unhappiness you can.

[*Enter* CHARLOTTE.]

CHARLOTTE. Ready.

JOHN. Right.

LOWRIE. Yes, I'll do that. I'll save her all the unhappiness I can. Yes, I will.

[*Exeunt together, up,* JOHN *and* CHAR-LOTTE.]

[*Goes to window.*] Mind the mill-pond, Chattie; Fly's frisky to-day, he tried to kick me when

c

I fed him, and if he shies when you're mounting
—oh, look out!

JOHN [*off*]. Go carefully, old girl!

CHARLOTTE [*off*]. All right! We must get a fence
put up, it's too close to the door to be safe.

[*Sound of departing horses. LOWRIE watches
at the window, hesitates, looks round the room,
and presently picks up a cushion and goes
slowly over to OWEN, holding it in front of
her with both hands. She stands in front of
him, holding it near his face. He is quite
unconscious of it. He whimpers: his cigarette
has gone out. LOWRIE puts down the cushion
and lights it again for him; picks up the
cushion and suddenly collapses with the cushion
on his knees, her head on it, sobbing.*]

LOWRIE. Oh, forgive me, Owen darling; you know
I love you or I wouldn't be able to do it! It's
for you and Phil both I'm going to do it.
[*OWEN strokes her hair affectionately, undis-
turbed.*] Do you think you'll struggle? I wonder
if being smothered hurts, if it is very horrible?
Oh, Owen, do forgive me! [*She stands up again
with the cushion: he throws away his cigarette
end and whimpers for another.*] Yes, I'll give
you another, and then count one, two, three
and do it. [*She gives him a cigarette; he catches
and strokes her hand; she kisses him.*] Owen, I

believe you know what I'm saying, and you
approve. Oh, you dear! You'll be able to see
and hear again in the place I'm sending you
to: perhaps you'll be a little boy again among
the angels, and there'll be Christ there and
all the most wonderful things: there'll be
angels, and harps and angels [*she is getting
more and more hysterical*] and golden crowns—
and one! two!——

[*Enter* PHILIPPA *L.*]

PHILIPPA. Lowrie, have you seen my scissors?

[LOWRIE *gasps and drops the cushion.*
PHILIPPA *rummages about, not taking much
notice of her. As she passes* OWEN, *stops and
pats his shoulder.* OWEN *takes her hand, then
drops it.*]

Isn't he strange? He always wants you, now,
Lowrie, to do everything; before, I used to be
the only person he would let touch him. I
wonder why.

LOWRIE [*still very agitated*]. I don't know.

PHILIPPA. Poor old chap. I'm sure he likes to feel
you're by him. [*Wanders out, L.*]

LOWRIE [*taking cloth off the table*]. Supposing she
had caught us doing it! What would you have
done, Owen? This will be better. It may be
good-bye for ever, because you're going to
heaven and I'm not sure God won't send me

to hell, but I don't care, I don't care—for
Phil's sake. Oh, I wonder if I can, now I'm
perfectly certain I ought to! Oh, God, help
me to do it! I'm very young and weak to
wilfully give my soul to be damned, but help
me to have strength to do it, for Phil's sake
and Chattie's, Amen—Three!

[*She twists the cloth round his head and pulls
at it madly.* OWEN *flings himself up from his
chair and catches her wrist. The cloth falls off
his head, but he is gasping, his face red and
full of animal terror.* LOWRIE *sinks down
behind the chair, but he keeps a hold on her
wrist over the back; she springs up wildly; he
gropes for her. Suddenly she slips free and
lies still on the floor a moment:* OWEN,
*whimpering excitedly, begins groping about for
her. She gets up and leans against the wall,
panting.*]

O God! help me! I can't do it! I can't kill him,
like in a dream! God, help me!

[OWEN *finds the door and gropes for the
handle, shaking with terror. It opens, and
enter* PHILIPPA.]

PHILIPPA. I'm sure I left them in here somewhere.
Why, what ever's the matter with Owen?

LOWRIE [*in a composed and unnatural voice: her
eyes are wide*]. I don't know.

PHILIPPA. Look at your hair! Has he been violent?

LOWRIE [*with a laugh, in a sort of hysterical calm*]. Owen violent! No! Fancy the old dear hurting anyone. [PHILIPPA *takes him by the shoulder, calming him*.] He fell asleep and had a bad dream or something, and jumped up suddenly in a fright.

[PHILIPPA *leads him back to his chair. He sits down still shaking, and when he realizes* PHILIPPA *is preparing to leave him, begins whimpering with terror again*.]

PHILIPPA. What on earth is he so terrified of?

LOWRIE. I can't think.

PHILIPPA [*disengaging* OWEN'S *hands*]. Call me if anything happens.

LOWRIE. All right. I can't think what's the matter with him. [*Exit* PHILIPPA.]

It's all over now, I must do it now, or you'd never trust me again and then they might guess. I must do it now, it's not the time to get weak-minded now. But I won't be so silly as to try strength again. [*Glancing at the window*.] The pond! [*She goes to front door, opens it, locks other door; suddenly throws the cloth over his head and springs back. He leaps up, pulling it off, blunders to door L., finds it locked, feels round the wall to the front door, and staggers out.* LOWRIE *slams the door behind him and goes to window.*]

LOWRIE. Pray God he may drown quickly, and not struggle like he did before.

> [*She kneels up at the window, silent and absolutely still for fully fifteen seconds. Suddenly she gives a half-scream and jumps back, covering her eyes. She turns towards the audience, her eyes covered, still gasping.*]

I mustn't scream, I mustn't scream, I mustn't scream. [*She drops her hands and stares about her.*] I mustn't scream, or they'll rescue him. I must wait. [*She stands still a moment, then goes to door L. and unlocks it; rearranges tablecloth.*]

> [*Re-enter* PHILIPPA.]

PHILIPPA. They were in my basket after—— Hallo, where's he gone?

LOWRIE [*in the same unnaturally calm manner*]. Out. He wanted to go, so I faced him to the paddock and let him.

PHILIPPA. I suppose he's all right. You're sure you got him facing properly?

LOWRIE. Quite. He's all right. I know he's quite all right.

PHILIPPA. Very well, only I'm a bit anxious about him because he seems queer to-day.—Do you think you can wear that frock another winter, dear?

LOWRIE. Frock? Yes, my frock's all right.

PHILIPPA. It's getting very short. I think I had better cut this one of mine down for you.

LOWRIE [*keeping on glancing at the window*]. Yes.

PHILIPPA. Let me measure you. Why, what's the matter? What are you so excited about?

LOWRIE. I'm not excited—I—I think he frightened me a bit. Look, there's John and Chattie coming back already.

PHILIPPA. Poor old thing!—I wonder what's wrong with him, he's a lamb generally.

LOWRIE. He didn't mean to—— Chattie's leading Fly, and he's stumbling. They must have had a spill, and that's why they have turned back. I do hope they haven't hurt poor Fly.

PHILIPPA [*glancing at the window across the room*]. He doesn't look very bad.

LOWRIE. No, I'm sure he's all right. I'm sure he's quite all right. [*She begins to laugh.*] Silly of me, I don't know what there is to laugh at in that: I know he's quite all right.

JOHN [*off*]. Help! Help!

LOWRIE. What's that?

PHILIPPA. Is one of them hurt?

LOWRIE [*quickly*]. Perhaps that's it.

PHILIPPA [*opens door up, gives a quick cry*]. Stay inside, Lowrie, and don't look out of the window! Promise me you won't look out of the window! [*Exit, closing door.* LOWRIE *comes forward and stands dry-eyed. Presently shuffling steps and voices outside.*]

PHILIPPA [*off*]. No, don't carry him inside, Lowrie's there.

JOHN [*off*]. Poor kid, she'll be terribly upset.

PHILIPPA [*off*]. Yes, but for his sake we can't be sorry: it was a merciful release to him.

JOHN [*off*]. Amen to that.

PHILIPPA [*off, breaking down*]. Oh, Owen, Owen, my little Owen! Nobody knew him as I did, when you were a beautiful little boy in holland overalls and we used to go exploring up the mill-stream together! I've been a bad sister to you, a cruel sister, I haven't treated you nearly as kindly as I ought, and now he's gone, and I can never do anything for him again! Oh, Owen, I didn't know how much I loved you!

[LOWRIE *suddenly collapses on the floor, weeping loudly.*]

JOHN [*off*]. She's heard! We may as well bring him in.

[*They open the door, and* CHATTIE *and* JOHN, *both quite composed, carry* OWEN'S *body in on a short ladder, his face covered in* JOHN'S *jacket. They bear him straight through the other door.* PHILIPPA *comes to* LOWRIE, *and kneels down beside her.*]

PHILIPPA. You dear, you're all I've got left now: Chattie will get married, and you and I will be all alone. But you mustn't cry for him: he is happy in heaven now. It was God's kind will to him to take him from his suffering. You know, dear, we couldn't wish him to live on as he was; his life was only a misery to him, and it is God's mercy that has released him. Always trust in God, Lowrie, and don't let your own rebellious thoughts interfere with His will. God's purpose is worked out in His own time, and though He may use the weakest of us sometimes as His instruments, it is not for us to anticipate His will: He accomplishes it without any help from us.

[*Re-enter* CHARLOTTE *and* JOHN.]

CHARLOTTE. I'm silly, but I can't help crying a bit. Yet I know it's all for the best.—I wish I hadn't talked like that, though: if I'd held my tongue a little longer, there'd have been no need. [*Dabs her eyes.*]

JOHN [*nervously*]. I feel for you, of course, in your bereavement; but we must admit it's all for the best.

PHILIPPA. Yes, John, you're right; it's the best thing for him.

LOWRIE. Phil?

PHILIPPA. Yes, darling.

LOWRIE. I do love you [*pause*]. It was the best thing, wasn't it?

PHILIPPA. Yes.

LOWRIE. Oh, Phil, I do feel awful. Can what's right make you feel awful like that? Did Chattie feel like that?

PHILIPPA. Like what, dear?

LOWRIE. I feel as if God hated me; I don't know why; I can't help it. Oh, I do feel so awful, Phil, I can't bear it.

PHILIPPA. What's the matter?

LOWRIE [*with an effort*]. Nothing. I can't tell you.

PHILIPPA. Do tell me.

LOWRIE. No, I can't: God would never forgive *that*—I *must* bear it. [*Stands up.*] I *will* bear it. I *won't* tell you. [*Walks down stage.*]

CHARLOTTE. What is the matter with her?

PHILIPPA. Sh! She'll tell us presently. She's too wrought up now, don't pay any attention to her.

JOHN. Shall I go now, Chattie? Is there anything else I can do?

PHILIPPA. No, don't go, John; stay a bit.

CHARLOTTE. Phil?

PHILIPPA. Yes?

CHARLOTTE. How did it happen? He doesn't generally go out in the afternoons, and anyhow when he's faced towards the paddock he generally goes straight there. Was he alone?

PHILIPPA. I don't know, Chattie; he was very excited and queer this afternoon. Lowrie started him off all right, she says.

CHARLOTTE. Do you think——? [*She pauses to suggest suicide.* LOWRIE *suddenly screams.*] You'd better make her go to bed, Phil, or she'll be ill.

PHILIPPA. I do *hope* it wasn't that.

[LOWRIE *screams again.*]

CHARLOTTE. He knew the pond was there, so he might have done it. You say he seemed very excited and queer.

PHILIPPA. Oh, Chattie, I hope he didn't: I'd be miserable all my life if I thought that was it. Oh, my poor Owen!

JOHN. There's no need to think that, Phil: let's take the charitable view. I can't believe he would be so wicked as to take his own life violently away.

CHARLOTTE. We had better question Lowrie.

PHILIPPA. No, don't, you'll only upset her worse.

CHARLOTTE. It can't be helped.—Lowrie! [LOWRIE *moves up a little, but keeps her face to the audience.*] Did you see him start?

LOWRIE. I saw him walk straight across to the water, and he was kicking with his legs, but he couldn't swim; only he went round and round in circles, and I couldn't look.

PHILIPPA. Lowrie!

JOHN. You saw him fall in?

PHILIPPA. Why didn't you call me? Why didn't you tell me? Oh, Lowrie, we might have saved him!

LOWRIE [*shaking her head*]. I couldn't tell you.

PHILIPPA. Oh, Lowrie, we might!

LOWRIE [*turning*]. No, Pippy dear; you said it was for the best, didn't you? You said he was happier now, and it was God's will: so why should you want to save him?

PHILIPPA. How can you say such wicked things!

LOWRIE. I'll tell you how I can say such wicked things, Pippy. It's because I killed him, that's why! I tried to kill him again and again, but I couldn't, because he was so strong and I was such a weak little fool. If only I had thought of drowning him at first, I could have done it easily, but in the end I had to frighten him, so that he did not know where he was going. I did it for you, Pippy, because I couldn't bear to see him spoiling your life, and Chattie not able to marry, and he living on in misery. I thought he would be glad to die, Pippy, but he wasn't; he hated it, he fought me. I never meant to tell, I meant to keep it secret, so as you and Chattie would be happy and free and not know; and even if God thought I was wrong and sent me to hell, perhaps you would never

know. But I'm a little fool, I couldn't bear it,
I had to blurt it out, and now it's all no good
and you will be unhappy all the same, because
you know.

> [JOHN *steps towards her and deliberately knocks her down.*]

JOHN. Murderer! Murderer! You, to kill your
own blind brother! [*She clings to his foot.*]
You snake, give up crawling around me!
[*Heaves her off his foot.*]

LOWRIE [*very low*]. Phil!

PHILIPPA. I can't speak to you yet, Lowrie.

> [*Exit hurriedly L.*]

LOWRIE. But I did it for you and Chattie, John.
Can't you see it was for Chattie I did it? So
as—you—get married?

JOHN. And d'you think I would marry into a
murderer's family? D'you think I would marry
the sister of a girl what's going to be '*ung*?

LOWRIE. Hung!

JOHN. Yes, when I've told the police, they'll come
and hang you, Lowrie; and may God have
mercy on your soul: though I doubt much if
He ought to.

CHARLOTTE. Will you tell?

LOWRIE. I'll go with you, John; I'll go to the
police quietly; I'd rather go than wait for them
to come and fetch me.

JOHN. You will not! Do you think I want my name dragged into a business like this, a dirty, foul business? You'll stay here! Christ, I'm afraid of the lightning dropping while you're about me! [*Moves to door up:* LOWRIE *follows him.*] Get inside! And don't you even exasperate the Lord by praying to Him. [*Exit:* LOWRIE *buries her face in a chair.*]

CHARLOTTE. John! [*She runs suddenly after him, calling, leaving the door open.*]

LOWRIE. It isn't true! It isn't true! I never did it, I never! Oh, I know I never did it, I couldn't do, I couldn't do it. I couldn't kill anything! Oh, Owen! He'll go telling lies and the police will come and hang me, and it's all a mistake, a dream, I never did it, I only dreamt it, it's all a dream! [*Kneels upright, putting her hands together.*] O God, it's a dream, isn't it? Kind God, let me wake up now. I've been dreaming long enough. O God, help me to wake up, and I'll never dare to go to sleep again, never, never! Oh, let me wake up! [*She bites the back of her hand and waits a moment, rigid, expectant, with her eyes shut: then suddenly opens them.*] I'm awake now, say I'm awake now. Say I dreamt it all about Owen, say I'm in bed; say he's all right! O God, I'm sure he's all right, I'm sure he's quite all right, I know he's quite all right—silly of me to laugh. [*Gets up, looking round the room.*] Owen! Owen! Where are you? They said you'd be able to hear and see again where you've gone to: you must hear me, you haven't died into the blackness, have you? [*She falls by the pool of water near the door.*] O wicked water, you know you're only a dream, aren't you? I didn't really see you dripping out of him—O wicked water, why won't you let me wake up? Owen, Owen! He's all right, only he can't hear me, and now John is telling lies, when it was all a dream! O Owen, come and save me! Owen!

[*She stands stock still, listening: there is silence for five seconds.* LOWRIE *runs to the door, opens it: there is nothing there. She gives a cry of delight, and crooks her arm exactly as before; comes back as if leading him to his chair by the fire.*]

LOWRIE. I *knew* it was only a dream!

QUICK CURTAIN

A COMEDY
OF GOOD AND EVIL

FOR ONE MUST ALWAYS BE CAREFUL
OF DISTINCTIONS!
Lao Tse

D

NOTE

THIS *Comedy* was first performed for the Three Hundred Club in London at the Court Theatre on July 6th, 1924. It was later produced at the Playhouse, Oxford, by Mr. J. B. Fagan, who brought it to London, where the first public performance opened at the Ambassador's Theatre on March 30th, 1925.

*

The persons, events, and doctrines described are imaginary. No reference is made to any living person, or the beliefs of any existing body of thought.

The accent is that of the South Snowdon district. The dialect is not intended for a translation of Welsh idiom, but for the English spoken, when occasion demands, by Welsh-speaking country people. Thus it varies considerably according to the speaker's education, and at its most fluent naturally approximates to written rather than spoken English.

The pronunciation of the Welsh words introduced is very easy, as the spelling is phonetic. The most important things to remember are that *w* is generally a vowel (oo), and that the other vowels approximate to the French (*not* Italian) usage, preserving their original sound in all diphthongs; that *ll* is simply an *l* loudly whispered instead of spoken, that *f* is our *v*, and *dd* is the spoken *th* (as in *the*), *ch* is pronounced much as in German, *r* is rolled, and *y* is generally like the *u* in *but*.

Bakehouse is pronounced ba-kooss.

Bach and *fach* are simply terms of endearment.

CHARACTERS

THE REV. JOHN WILLIAMS, *Rector of Cylfant*: An elderly stocky man with a Celtic face: Greek nose, big spiny eyebrows, small wide eyes of great brilliance; a short grey beard on the front of his chin; his black clothes worn paper-thin; wooden clogs.

He has great natural dignity of movement.

When he talks to himself it is in a rapid rhythmic recitative punctuated by explosions. He talks chiefly to himself.

His Welsh accent is very noticeable, but attractive.

On no account must the audience be allowed to laugh at him.

MINNIE, *his wife*: Younger, but not young; a repressed face—protruding eyes. An astonishing capacity for putting speech in a dramatic form, regardless of its content: a tendency accentuated by extreme difficulty with the English language. Manner abstracted. She thinks as a grasshopper jumps. No education. A wooden leg.

The couple are incredibly poor, even for clergy of the Church of England in Wales. (This is, of course, before their position was improved by Disestablishment.)

GLADYS: A blue-eyed, golden-haired child; as

young as is technically convenient (ten, at the most). Notable for an unearthly innocence of expression. Her English accent is unimpeachable, and she gives every sign of a most careful upbringing, as well as of a naturally nice disposition.

SCRAGGY EVAN THE POST: A crab-like postman, in semi-uniform.

OWAIN FLATFISH: Very disreputable. He is incredibly dirty and ragged, and one end of his moustache hangs two inches below the other.

MARI JONES, GRANDDAUGHTER BAKEHOUSE: About nineteen, pretty and clumsy in her movements, altogether untrained and easily influenced.

MRS. JONES BAKEHOUSE, *her grandmother*: About sixty, good-looking and of good carriage and manner. Has probably been in service when young and seen the world.

TIMOTHY YSGAIRNOLWEN: A young Saxonate, town-trained. But his accent is quite noticeable, especially when excited.

MR. GAS JONES: A retired plumber of great tact.

MRS. RESURRECTION JONES, *a miracle*: A stout, red woman of fifty with a deep bass voice and a majestic manner.

SCENE

A RATHER poky little Welsh kitchen: ugly and spotless; full of furniture—varnished deal with a mixture of a little good old oak. Door to street up L., window, smothered in curtains and geraniums, up centre; stairs leading from below fire-place R., harmonium L.; fire of the "half open" sort R., with big chair above it. Table centre, with lamp. Books, photographs, and illuminated certificates (Welsh) in incredible numbers. Under the window is an oak chest with a large zinc bowl on it, and a mangle R.

A COMEDY
OF GOOD AND EVIL

ACT I

Before the curtain rises MINNIE *is heard practising hymns on the harmonium. (A piece for the orchestra should be chosen which will present a suitable contrast to this.) As it rises,* MR. WILLIAMS *is discovered sitting by the fire, darning his surplice:* MINNIE *playing.*

Time, September, 9 P.M.

MINNIE [*She has finished the verse. Trying several different Amens:*] *A*men!—A-amen! *A*men!

MR. WILLIAMS [*laying his darning in his lap, and gesticulating very gently with his spectacles*]. I am a very sinful man, Minnie: a very sinful man. Temptation is always lurking ready for us. It is hard. Hard. [*Long pause: then loud and sudden as a whip-crack:*] Hard!

MINNIE [*getting it at last; taking no notice*]. A-a-a-amen!

MR. WILLIAMS. You can't use that one, Minnie: in the church harmony-um the middle C is missing. [*Puts on spectacles and threads a new needle.*]

MINNIE. And I can't practise the other, because *this* harmony-um she not having F-sharp.

MR. WILLIAMS [*to himself*]. It is a grand, terrible thing to be a humble soldier, fighting the shadowy battles of the Lord: fighting for the forces Good against the forces Evil. Yes. But there are times when it is not easy to tell which is which. [*Shakes his head.*] It is a great lesson to humility, that. [*Almost trumpeting:*] It were easy to fight, and you certain! Certain! [*Softly:*] But it is not ease that one should be looking for in that battle. Certainty, she is the mother of pride. Ease, he is the father. And we hitting in the dark, and praying that the blow may find an enemy, not a friend. Is he not a strange thing, Minnie, Pride—that enemy who grows strong by *our* victories, is weakened by our defeats? The enemy, riding among us on his tall horse, triumphing over the strong, fleeing from the weak, the vanquished, the sinner? It is he alone, of all the powers of hell, that can strike at the martyr at the stake: and strike more terribly, more mortally, I am thinking, than on any other occasion.

MINNIE [*without any particular comprehension*]. Isn't the love of Heaven will save you?

MR. WILLIAMS [*crooking his hand to his ear*]. Ah?

MINNIE [*no louder*]. Isn't the love of Heaven will save you, whatever?

MR. WILLIAMS [*vaguely: he still has not heard*]. Ah.

MINNIE. Amen! A-amen! [*Sniffs; pause; then suddenly begins to sing with accuracy and passion:*]

> O Love, who ere life's earliest dawn
> On me Thy choice hast gently laid,
> O Love, who here as Man was born
> And wholly like to us wast made,
> O Love, I give myself to Thee;
> Thine ever, only Thine to be.

[*She stops, staring in a fixed way: then gives a sudden sniff and tries Amens again: then quite suddenly:*] That is the grand, beautiful hymn.

MR. WILLIAMS. There are times when I say to my soul: Life is simple: do that which is right. Then my soul answers within me: What is Right?—How shall I answer my soul?

MINNIE. It is all in the Bible. [*Pause.*] Somewhere.

MR. WILLIAMS. Ah. But I cannot find it.

MINNIE [*vaguely*]. You have a concordance. [*Pause; staring in front of her, and speaking apparently to the harmonium:*] It will be a grand day for me when I see the gates of Jerusalem open, and feel the balm of the Heavenly Love. [*Sniffs.*] And me wearing a robe of purple and gold. [*Sniffs again.*] And having two legs.

MR. WILLIAMS [*returning to his own train of*

thought]. Humility . . . ah, yes! Humility.
[*Rapidly, half under his breath:*] Even the
angels of God, they too give us example of
humility. Isaiah tells us that they have six
wings, [*voice rising*] but do they use them all
for His service? No! No! With twain they
cover their head, and with twain they cover
their feet, and with twain do they fly. Four for
humility, two for use, Minnie: then ought we
not also to devote our talents to humility and
to service in the same proportion as the angels
give us example?

MINNIE [*singing*].

> Rock of Ages, cleft for me,
> Let me hide myself in Thee—

[*Breaks off, turns, and stares at* MR. W. *With
sudden passion.*] Mr. Williams, there's a grand
Christian you are, indeed! You preach better
than any bard, you do, sir—fair play to you!
[*Then, as if half ashamed of the outburst:*]
A-men!—I cannot find a good Amen, not in
the book, anywhere. [*Speaking into the harmonium:*] There was three schoolmasters in
church last Sunday: one of them Intermediate.
And they coming in bicycles, special!

MR. WILLIAMS. Ah! Indeed! Three!

MINNIE [*bitterly*]. And not one other person else,

neither: leaving Timothy Ysgairnolwen, that is turn out of his chapel for going to the big whist drive at Beddgelert. And he not caring for the grand preaching, neither: he only thinking the Church safer for his soul than give up religion altogether. Ah, they are proud of it, them chapels! And they thinking it a great shame in a village to have many church-peoples! [*In supreme derision of the worldliness implied:*] They, with their ministers in motor-bicycles!

MR. WILLIAMS. I'm thinking, Minnie, wouldn't it be time I did the washing?

MINNIE. Is she boil?

MR. WILLIAMS. Ah.

MINNIE [*coaxingly*]. Wouldn't I be doing it, John bach? There's hard you working.

MR. WILLIAMS. No, indeed! And you with a weak heart and only one leg to you? Who ever heard!

MINNIE. But, John bach, I not washing with my leg! And my heart, she very good to-day.

MR. WILLIAMS. Is it not the husband's business to make the money?

MINNIE. It is.

MR. WILLIAMS. Me, to be letting my wife do washing for money! Wasn't it agreed, when I refused the church in Bangor, that I should do a little work, extra?

MINNIE. Yes, but——

MR. WILLIAMS. And why should I not do washing? What else should I do?

MINNIE. You might be writing for the papers, or teaching the language to some old Saxon.

MR. WILLIAMS. Washing is better paid, and more useful! Besides, Minnie fach, there is great virtue to humility in washing: they say the Pope is once a year washing the feet of beggars. So why should not I wash the clothes for the summer visitors?

MINNIE. Fifteen pounds a year! It's little the Church gives us, fair play to it! I would like to see one of they chapel deacons living on fifteen pounds a year and a rectory!—They do say, Mr. Williams, that some of they clergy in England are so rich they do be *living* in their rectories, 'stead of letting them! Did you ever hear that! And we living in a little bwythyn with two rooms in it!

[*Meanwhile* MR. W. *has risen, taken off his black coat carefully, taken off his white cuffs— he is wearing an army shirt—rolled up his sleeves, and is trying to tie an apron round his great waist.*]

MR. WILLIAMS. Where is the soap, Minnie?

MINNIE. Behind the tea-pot. [MR. W. *does not move: he is suddenly rapt in meditation. Louder:*] Behind the tea-pot!

MR. WILLIAMS [*vaguely*]. Behind the tea-pot? [*Goes uncertainly to the mantelpiece, and feels behind the tea-pot; takes out a cake of yellow soap. Stares at it a moment; then suddenly remembering:*] Soap? Ah, yes, soap. Soap. [*Begins the wash.*]

MINNIE. It is a great peety, and you not accepting they great church in Bangor. Wouldn't she be very handy, she, for the great preaching? Really?

MR. WILLIAMS [*to himself, in a rapid recitative, pausing and gazing up with a shirt in his hands*]. It is generally supposed that He passed the three days before His resurrection in the pale kingdoms of death. No. No. What did He say to the repentant thief? This day shalt thou be with Me in Paradise! *This day!* It is therefore beyond doubt that He passed straight to heaven with no sojourn among the dead.

MINNIE [*louder*]. Mr. Williams bach! It's I'm thinking it great peety you not preaching in the big church in Bangor she was offer!

MR. WILLIAMS. The Presence is with us, Minnie, wherever we are.

MINNIE. Isn't that what I'm saying? Wouldn't it

be with us in Bangor same as Cylfant? The
Lord is no respecter of persons, John. He
wouldn't neglect a famous preacher any more
than a poor country "parch," would He?

MR. WILLIAMS. Ah!

MINNIE. It's burying your talent in the garden you
are!

MR. WILLIAMS [*moved by sudden emotion*]. Ah!
That parable by false interpretation is blamed
for all man's spiritual pride!—With twain they
covered their heads, and with twain they
covered their feet, and with twain they did fly.

MINNIE [*rising and filling a small kettle, which she
puts on the fire*]. It's the *grand* Christian you are,
Mr. Williams!

MR. WILLIAMS. No! No, don't say that.

MINNIE [*half to herself, her expression curiously
twisted*]. It's a bad wicked little wife I am to
you, I'm thinking, fair play to me. [*Sniffs;
takes enamelled pail, opens front door, and
stumps out into the darkness with it. MR. W.
goes on washing a few moments. A party go
down the street, singing "The Ash Grove" in
parts. MR. W. pauses, and feels under his apron
for his watch; then suddenly in vexation:*]

MR. WILLIAMS. Ah! To goodness gracious!
Ah, me!

[*Re-enter MINNIE with pail filled; during*

the next few speeches she and MR. W. *stagger to the door with the wash-tub and pour the water out into the street, then* MR. W. *rinses the clothes in fresh water and finally begins to put them through the mangle, while* M. *busies herself about the room.*]

MINNIE [*slowly*]. I'm thinking it's a great peety we haven't got a lit-tle cat.

MR. WILLIAMS [*to himself*]. Ah, to goodness it's the great loss!

MINNIE. It would be company for us, the long evenings. [*Sentimentally:*] I would like a little cat, really, to be talking to.

MR. WILLIAMS. It must have fallen off in the street, Minnie. The ring was getting very old.

MINNIE. What is it?

MR. WILLIAMS. It's my father's little gold cross, that I carried on my chain.

MINNIE. You've lost it?

MR. WILLIAMS. Ah.

MINNIE. It is a great peety. But it's too dark to be looking for it to-night. Try you in the morning. Someone will find it, p'r'aps.

MR. WILLIAMS. It is a terrible loss.

MINNIE. They do say you can't lose a cross. They say they always finding her, some day. She coming home. [*Mysteriously:*] They say when a cross going away, she going on an errand!

E

She have something to do! When she finishing, she coming home. They saying that! [*Sniffs.*] But I would *love* a little cat, John bach!

MR. WILLIAMS. Ah?

MINNIE. I *would* like a little cat, to be talking to. A little black one with a blue ribbon. And a little bell.—Or a little dog, perhaps; but they dirty in the house—or p'r'aps a little girl.

MR. WILLIAMS. Little cats steal, Minnie fach. And dogs get distemper. And little girls lead to *terrible* expenses also.

MINNIE. Ooo! I knew one, *wicked* she was. What she do? Did you ever hear that, Mr. Williams? Listen you! My aunt, if she having pieces bacon left over, she putting them in the little oven; and when tea-time she opens the door; and the plate coming out; and what is on it? [*Dramatically:*] *Little Pieces Bacon!* [*Pause for effect.*] Oh, but Jinnie she *awfully* wicked! One day my aunt, she open the door, and plate coming out; and what is on it? *Nothing at all!* Then my uncle, they saying: "Look in Jinnie's bed." And my aunt, she look in Jinnie's bed, and what is there? [*Triumphantly:*] *Little pieces bacon!* Oh, she was wicked! She couldn't eat them all, look you, but she *biting* them! My uncle, they terribly angry. Oh, they a *strong* man, my uncle: they was very strong in the tongue. But they not saying a word: they just taking Jinnie by the neck; and what did they do? They *drowned* her in the pond! Did you ever hear that, Mr. Williams?

MR. WILLIAMS. Dear me! To goodness! He was a hard man!

MINNIE. Ooo, he was that! And my aunt, she not daring say a word! Oh, he was terribly strong in the mouth. But I don't *hold* with doing a thing like that, eh, Mr. Williams?

MR. WILLIAMS. No, indeed!

MINNIE. Oh, and she was pretty too! But she was wicked. But if *I* having a little cat, I having her very little; and when she steal, what do I do? I smack her! And when she steal again, what do I do? I smack her! Then, p'r'aps, when she getting a big cat, she not stealing at all! There's very lonely we are sometimes, John bach: we could do with a little cat, to be friendly with. And I sitting and thinking there's no one to be caring for us, we dying stiff in our bed. [*Sitting down:*] It wouldn't be a great surprise to me, John, was the Lord to send an angel to us in disguise.

MR. WILLIAMS [*stupefied*]. Now whatever for would He do that?

MINNIE. I don't know . . . but it might happen. You never know.

MR. WILLIAMS. May He have mercy on us, and not put us in so difficult a position, greatly above our station!

MINNIE. A great, uncommon, shiny one, p'r'aps: same as she came to Mary. Or got up all ugly, like Owain Flatfish that does catching fish in the mud with the double joints of his great toes. You never know.—Or like a little child. —Or, p'r'aps, even, like a little cat.

MR. WILLIAMS. But why should an angel be coming to us, Minnie?

MINNIE. Oh . . . I don't know . . . but she *might*. You never know . . . and we . not seeing many visitors . . . except Mrs. Jones Shop, and Mrs. Jones Bakehouse, and Mr. Gas Jones . . . and p'r'aps the Post-Office Daughter, and the Butchery Aunt, though it's seldom they coming near us . . . and Mrs. Resurrection Jones, when she not having fits. . . . Oh, if it was a stranger coming to us, it's hard I would be looking at him, that's truth, Mr. Williams Church!

MR. WILLIAMS. That is a very presumptuous idea you have got in your head, indeed.

MINNIE [*quite carried away by her idea; in a rapt ecstatic voice:*] And what would we be giving him, whatever? Is it bread and jam? No! Is it bacon? No! Is it tea? No! Well, then, is it

milk and honey? No! it isn't milk and honey!
What would we give her, then? *We would
bring her butter in a lordly dish!* [*Triumphant
pause; then with complete collapse of emotion:*]
Don't you be breaking the buttons on pants
The Royal Goat in the mangle, John!

MR. WILLIAMS [*to himself, mechanically turning
the mangle*]. We are told that Og, king of
Bashan, had a bedstead of iron. It is therefore——

MINNIE [*jumping up, almost screaming, and seizing
the pants*]. Do you be minding buttons pants
Royal Goat——

MR. WILLIAMS [*stopping*]. Buttons!—Ah, yes,
buttons. Buttons.—There's careless I am, girl
fach.

MINNIE [*having saved the buttons, sitting down
again*]. But p'r'aps it's just like any other
stranger we should be using him, John: would
that be right? Giving him a cup of tea, with a
bit of bread and butter to it?

MR. WILLIAMS [*straightening his back with difficulty and turning*]. When the three angels
came to Abraham in the plains of Mamre,
he said: My Lord, let a little water, I pray
you, be fetched, and wash your feet, and rest
yourselves under the tree. And I will fetch a
morsel of bread, and comfort ye your hearts.

And in the New Testament yr Arglwydd said:
Even as ye do it to the least of these little
ones, ye do it unto Me. It is therefore evident
that the virtue of the act does not lie in the
divine nature of the stranger but in the
hospitable intention of the giver.

MINNIE. Would it make no difference at all, then,
to our chances heaven, was it a real angel or
was it Owain Flatfish himself we giving a
cup of tea to?

MR. WILLIAMS. No. No. It would make no difference at all, whoever it might be, so be he
seemed in need of our assistance.

MINNIE [*slowly*]. That is a great peety.—But I
would *rather* it was an angel all the same, Mr.
Williams bach! It would feel more sure certain,
whatever . . . at least, he not being possibly
for the worse, and possibly for the better. . . .
It isn't easy to believe, that, that she not making
any little tiny slip of difference, if she be an
angel herself or if she be Owain Flatfish Dwl.
No, I can't hardly believe that. Oh, I would
love to see a great, shining angel, that's truth!
[*The voice of a child singing happily something
un-Celtic but strange (such as "Sam Hall") heard
in the far distance.*] What's that? [*She opens the
door and listens, moving her head from side to side
like a hen.*] There's grand singing it is, indeed.

Who ever heard? [*Shuts door and comes down stage;* MR. W. *has finished the mangling and put on his coat and sits down by the fire.* M. *sits on harmonium stool, facing him.*] Has Timothy Ysgairnolwen sent in the banns of marriage yet to Mari Bakehouse, John bach?

MR. WILLIAMS. No.

MINNIE. I wish he would hurry, then! Or p'r'aps they'll be letting him back to Ebenezer, and Church missing a good marriage. Oh, she's a lovely little girl, Mari Bakehouse, the darling! I should like to see her married Church, really. But it's not so lovely as her granny used to she is, I'm thinking. Oh, she's a grand woman, Mrs. Jones Bakehouse, I'm thinking, for all she's one of they Albanian Baptists. Do you know what they're saying, Mr. Williams? They Albanian Baptists is building a chapel at Cylfant? They saying that! And a chapel to hold two hundred people! And they not more nor five families in the Parish! Did you ever hear!

MR. WILLIAMS [*to himself*]. Flesh! Flesh! Ah, it is a grievous burden not easily to be borne, laid like a heavy load across the back of the spirit. Ah! Ah! And to-morrow I must do the ironing, and my back aches terribly with the ironing. Ah, me!

MINNIE [*in quiet satisfaction*]. It's mortgaged out to the door-step they'll be, just like their betters!

> [*A child's scream, full of terror, is heard close outside the door.*]

Duw anwyl, what's that? [*Opens door.*] Pwy sydd 'na? Ooooo! [*This sound is a short O drawn out on a rising note, like the noise made by a self-conscious hen when stared at.*] Tyd yma, the poor darling!—Oh, there's bad she is, John, awful bad! [*Lifts the child over the threshold.*] Dead, p'r'aps! Oh, but she heavy! [*Leaving her on the floor by door.*]

MR. WILLIAMS. Well, to gracious!

MINNIE [MINNIE *is seized by a violent fit of coughing. Then:*] Ooo, the darling!

MR. WILLIAMS. Run you and get a feather to burn, quick. [*Exit* MINNIE, *stairs:* THE CHILD *sits up and has a look round;* MR. W. *rises, and she promptly lies flat again. He laboriously flicks water on her from the pail, which she bears without flinching. He too coughs once or twice. Re-enter* MINNIE *with a bottle.*] Have you found a feather?

MINNIE. I haven't, then; but here's this Universal Embrocation: was we giving her a little in a spoon, mightn't she be very good?

MR. WILLIAMS. Is she hurt?

MINNIE. I don't know that, she don't look; but it was a great uncommon wailing she make.—I'm thinking, why not smack her with a pair of they wet pants?

MR. WILLIAMS. Ah! Look, she's burnt her knee.

MINNIE. Oooo so! Now, how ever did she do that?

MR. WILLIAMS. Bring a little butter, and a rag.

MINNIE [*doing so; to herself:*] "And brought him butter in a——" Oooo, who ever—— [*Stops suddenly, her eyes dancing with mystery.*]

MR. WILLIAMS. Here, Minnie. [*He dresses the knee gently and clumsily.*]

MINNIE [*to herself*]. Glory! Glory! Glory!—Selah. [*Aloud:*] Do you help me bring her in the warm.

[*Together they carry her and lay her in the big chair.*]

MR. WILLIAMS. Gracious me! What a lovely little thing!

MINNIE. Ooo, she is that! [*They stare at her a moment. She opens a pair of wide innocent eyes, and then yawns indecently.*] Oh, the darling! Lie you quiet, 'nghariad. . . . Sir! —Is she boil?

MR. WILLIAMS. Ah.

MINNIE [*in suppressed triumph*]. Wouldn't we make her a cup of tea?

MR. WILLIAMS. Ah. [*He takes down the pot;* MINNIE *makes the tea*.] The poor little thing! Who is she?

MINNIE. Wouldn't we be giving her bit bread and butter?

MR. WILLIAMS. Perhaps, yes.

   [*He goes to cut it.* THE CHILD *crosses her legs and scratches her ear dreamily*.]

MINNIE. Do you take sugar, dear?

THE CHILD. If you please.

MINNIE. Here you are, sir.—Be quick with the bread and butter, John bach.

THE CHILD. Thank you very much.

MINNIE. Mind you don't burn your mouth; there's hot it is!

   [THE CHILD *takes no notice and drinks it with relish.* M. *takes the bread and butter from* MR. W. *and gives it her*.]

THE CHILD. Thank you.

MINNIE. Is it better you feeling?

THE CHILD. Yes, thank you.

   [M. *surreptitiously takes down a Bible and lays it on the table*.]

MR. WILLIAMS [*to himself*]. Poor thing, poor little thing! It is difficult to imagine where she can have come from. She talks perfect English. Perhaps she is belonging to one of the summer visitors.

MINNIE. John, there's buttering the air you are, not the loaf!

MR. WILLIAMS [*continuing*]. But what is she doing out so late at night? They ought to take proper care. She might have met with a serious accident.

MINNIE [*struggling with her memory, to herself*]. "My Lord, let a little . . ." [*Aloud:*] Would you like another cup nice tea, dear?—"To—to—comfort your heart?"

THE CHILD. If you please. [M., *in giving it, makes a little bob-curtsy*.] Thank you.

MINNIE. Are you not talking Welsh, sir?

THE CHILD. No. I am afraid I don't.

MINNIE [*in surprise*]. That is a great peety! I should have thought you would talk Welsh there, really, sir. Mr. Williams he like a hare: you know a hare is male one month, one month female? You know that, my dear? Mr. Williams talking Welsh one month and English another, so he not forgetting, sir, that why; but oh, I do *long* for a little bit talk Welsh after a few days of the English, that's truth I do! I wouldn't say one word of the old English if he would let me, really I wouldn't! And I hoping you would talk Welsh like any other child.

THE CHILD. I'm very sorry.

MINNIE. Now, if I was having a little cat, I talking Welsh to her all the time! No one would expect a poor little cat to understand the English, would they, sir?—Is the tea good?

THE CHILD. Yes, thank you.

MINNIE [*shrilly*]. John, there's the whole loaf you've cut into bread and butter, and there not another loaf in the house!

MR. WILLIAMS. Ah! There's an old silly I am! I'm very sorry! What a silly! Ah, indeed! [*In genuine distress.*]

MINNIE [*in contrition, aside to* MR. W.]. Mr. Williams bach, I didn't mean to be telling hard words to you, and before a stranger; and I not holding with a wife telling bad words to a man. There's a bad woman I am! And now I to go and do it in front of *him*, when I haven't said such wicked words, not for a month, have I, sir?

MR. WILLIAMS. Children don't notice, Minnie.

MINNIE. *Children*, John! Is it really a child you think he is? Didn't you see the light that was on him, out in the road, all blue and lovely? Was there ever a *child* had such a beautiful face, such eyes, the darling? There's blind you're getting! There isn't no human innocence had the eyes like that, bless him!

MR. WILLIAMS [*turning and gazing fixedly at* THE CHILD, *who is oblivious*]. Ah!

MINNIE. There's *me* was right, John bach: he's *come*, he has!

MR. WILLIAMS. Arglwydd trugarhâ wrthym!

[THE CHILD *turns and looks fixedly at* M. *and* MR. W.]

MINNIE [*under her breath*]. Glory, glory, glory!

MR. WILLIAMS. Arglwydd trugarhâ wrthym!

MINNIE. Gogoniant yn y goruchaf!

[*Tense pause;* THE CHILD *rises to her feet, slowly, and in doing so her hand accidentally touches the Bible on the table. She screams with agony, putting her fingers to her mouth; at the moment of contact a distinct cloud of smoke rises;* MR. W. *and* M. *both cough violently*.]

THE CHILD. Blast your eyesight, woman, can't you be careful with that book! [THE CHILD *is grinning with pain; the hair over her ears falls back, showing them to be pointed*.]

MINNIE [*her voice broken with coughing*]. Duw anwyl! John, it's a dev——

MR. WILLIAMS [*quickly*]. It's a *stranger*, Minnie!

[*Pause; both sides facing each other*.]

MINNIE [*suddenly springs forward; in a high shrill voice like a woman shooing a neighbour's chickens out of her kitchen, so fast the words are almost indistinguishable*]. Cerr'! Cerr'! Out of it! Get you away along out of it! Out of my kitchen, you! Coosht! Shoo! Shoo! Shoo! [*waving an arm*]. [*Pause;* THE CHILD *does not move. Suddenly* MINNIE *seizes the Bible and rushes at her; she springs out of the chair and leaps on to the window-sill among the geraniums, wrapping herself in the lace curtains, spitting at* MINNIE: *her face distorted with terror and rage.*] Away along out of it, you! Get along! Get along! Out of my kitchen, diawl i ti! Cerr' at dy dad, diawl i ti!

MR. WILLIAMS [*sternly*]. Minnie!

MINNIE [*slowly; trembling*]. Oh, the wicked, wicked great hypocrite! And me thinking it was an angel! [*Bursts into tears, still threatening with the Bible.*]

MR. WILLIAMS. Put that Bible back on the shelf! [*She moves almost unconsciously to obey.*] May Heaven forgive your cruelty, wife; for It knew you didn't mean harm! Can't you see you're *hurting* the poor thing?

MINNIE [*indignantly*]. And why isn't there hurting it I'd be?

MR. WILLIAMS [*softly*]. Is it a Christian, Minnie, would be hurting any living thing? Even a fly on the wall? And if he wouldn't wilfully hurt a fly on the wall, Minnie, whose feelings cannot be very acute, surely he wouldn't hurt such a highly organized and sensitive creature as that? As sensitive as ourselves, girl fach, if not more so.

MINNIE [*slowly*]. You mean you'd expect me to be gentle to a devil out of hell? [*Quickly:*] She's one of God's enemies, John, and if we harbour God's enemies there's damned we shall be!

MR. WILLIAMS. God's enemies are *our* enemies too, Minnie?

MINNIE. Yes, surely!

MR. WILLIAMS. And are we not taught to *love* our enemies, Minnie fach? Is there any exception made to that law?

MINNIE. Well, indeed!

MR. WILLIAMS. I think we should love them all, Minnie.—And are you sure it was so disinterested, your anger against her? Wasn't there personal disappointment in it, too?

MINNIE [*piteously*]. But she can't ever be *grateful* to us, John; she will return us evil for good, yes, indeed!

MR. WILLIAMS. If we do good in the hope of gratitude, Minnie, we have our reward! It's good with no hope of gratitude, no hope of return, no thought of danger to ourselves that is the good really!—Didn't I say that it was not the divine nature of the guest that

made Abraham's hospitality a virtue? Then
why should the infernal nature of the guest
affect the virtue of *our* hospitality?

MINNIE [*incredulously*]. You mean—you mean you
will *keep* him, Mr. Williams?

MR. WILLIAMS. I mean—[*breaking down and burying his face in his hands*] I mean I do not know
what to do indeed whatever! [*Silent pause,
MINNIE and THE CHILD watching him as
anxiously as a couple of dogs. Slowly he raises
his head.*] Bring me another bit of rag, Minnie.
[*She does so. He smears it in butter and, going
over slowly, in dead silence, bandages THE
CHILD's burnt hand.*]

MINNIE [*shakily*]. Did you notice the shape of the
burn on her knee?

MR. WILLIAMS. No.

MINNIE. Like that! [*Drawing a cross in the air.*]
There's a strange errand your little gold cross
went on, I'm thinking! She stumbling on it,
in the dark!

MR. WILLIAMS. Ah! Then it is I was to blame
that she took hurt! [*He helps her off the
window-sill. She is still shaking with fright.*]
Sit you down, girl fach! [*She sits in the big
chair again.*]

MINNIE [*very slowly*]. There's right, you, I'm
thinking, p'r'aps, John; whoever would have

thought!—The poor lost thing! It's a dangerous place Wales is for her, and she not even knowing the language! There's not much kindness she'd meet with, that's truth, and she coming to the house of one of they chapel ministers! There's the *grand* Christian you are, John, really!—Girl fach, there's truly sorry I am! I didn't think! [THE CHILD *smiles*.] And what shall we be calling her, John? Is it Gwenhyvar? No! Is it Gwenhydwy? No! Is it Blodwen, or Mair? No! [*Coaxingly:*] John, wouldn't we call her Gladys? It's a beautiful name, that! [*Sentimentally:*] If I had a little daughter of my own, John dear, there's Gladys I would be calling her!

CURTAIN

F

ACT II

SCENE: *The same, but* GLADYS *is asleep on the floor down stage L. by harmonium, in a bed made of rugs, red flannel petticoats, and other oddments. The blind is still down.*

TIME: *The following morning, half past seven. Daylight outside.*

Enter MINNIE *from stairs, in curling-papers. She has now two legs: the old one as before, with thick ankle, loose cotton stocking, and clog; the new one elegant, seductive: in silk stocking and Paris shoe, altogether à la* Vie Parisienne. *She walks somewhat gingerly, as if her control of the new limb was still a little imperfect. Her expression varies from delight via mystification to misgiving.*

She lets up the blind; then, turning towards the audience, raises her skirt a little to admire the new leg.

MINNIE. Well, I never! And where was you coming from, leg bach? [*Dubiously:*] There's strange you are! [*Running an appreciative thumb down the calf:*] Oooo, but you are lovely! [*Dubiously again:*] I wonder, now, is that the sort of leg they would be giving me in heaven?

[*During this speech* GLADYS *sits up in bed and regards her seriously.*]

GLADYS. Good morning.

MINNIE [*starting, a little ashamed*]. Good morning, you. [*She lets the skirt drop and lights the fire, as if there was nothing odd. Pause.*]

GLADYS. Shall I get up yet?

MINNIE. No, wait you till Mr. Williams is down. Then you can go up and dress.

[*Another pause.*]

GLADYS. Can I help you?

MINNIE [*kindly*]. No, indeed, Gladys fach, there's no need. Lie you quiet a bit. Was you sleep good?

GLADYS. Yes, thank you. [*Pause. Politely:*] That's a nice leg you've got, Mrs. Williams.

MINNIE [*distantly*]. Oh, she's not so bad.

GLADYS. Do tell me where you got it.

MINNIE. Little girls not ask too many questions. [*Rising and opening front door:*] There's fine day! [*Throughout the rest of the play the new leg exhibits a distinct and slightly improper personality of its own. Now, when* MINNIE *attempts to carry the mats outside, it begins to jib and shy like a frightened horse.*] Stea—dy, leg bach! Stea—dy! Wo! Hold up, then, you silly! [*She seizes the door-post to balance herself, the leg continuing to kick violently.*] Quiet, you!

Quiet! What's the matter with you, then? I'm only wanting shake the mats! What's all the trouble, then?—That's right, leg bach, quiet you! [*The leg comes to a standstill, but, when she again tries to pass the threshold, goes mad again.*] Oooo, that's the trouble, is it? There's no mistaking where *you* come from, I'm afraid; and that's truth!—Well, quiet you now: she not hurting you. [*She drops the mats, and with great difficulty sidles through the door, picking up the rector's little gold cross, which is lying outside.*] Ah, so you coming home, Cross bach? [*She looks at it a long time in silent disapproval, as a Prime Cause; then:*] Ah, well, the Lord's will be done. [*She lays it on the chest.*]

GLADYS. Hadn't you better put it away somewhere safe?

MINNIE. Who would be taking her then?

GLADYS. No one. But they're dangerous things to leave about.

MINNIE. That's true, indeed! [*She puts it in the drawer of the table, then looks at* GLADYS *steadily.*] Gladys, do you know what I am thinking? Shall I tell you, then? Very well, I will tell you. I thinking you know great deal more about my leg! I think you knowing where she coming from, and you not telling, Gladys

Diawl! There's wicked little girl you are, you not telling!

GLADYS. Did it hurt you very much when you had the old one cut off, Mrs. Williams?

MINNIE. Oh, it hurt awful!

GLADYS. Poor Mrs. Williams! It must be terrible to have a leg cut off. To see the doctor waiting with a big knife, and having the chloroform stuff, and not knowing whether you're going to wake up again alive. I should die of fright, I think.—Does it hurt terribly?

MINNIE [*her face darkened by memory*]. Oh, awful bad!

GLADYS. But that's the worst of legs, isn't it? I mean, if you want to be rid of them you've got to have them cut off, haven't you? You can't just say "Shoo! shoo!" to them, and they're gone, can you?

MINNIE. There's legs and there's legs.

GLADYS. Yes: but they'll none of them come off without cutting.

MINNIE. Ah, p'r'aps. [*Pause; then with great determination:*] If thy hand offend thee, cut it off and cast it from thee!

GLADYS. What was the matter with your first leg, then?

MINNIE. It had the inflammation.

GLADYS. And were you ill with it long, or

did the doctor cut it off as soon as it got
bad?

MINNIE. Ooo, months it was! Years, and me a
little girl, not able to go to school, not play, not
anything. The old doctor, he hoping to save
her! He not cutting her till she nearly dropping
off, that's truth, fair play to him!

GLADYS. How funny doctors are! You'd think they
hated cutting anything off!—I'd have thought
they'd like to do it when it was all nice and
new, instead of waiting till there was hardly
anything left worth cutting, wouldn't you?—
But they're like that! If I was to go to
a doctor and ask him to cut my arms off,
do you know I believe he'd refuse to
do it!

MINNIE. Is that so, really?

GLADYS. Mm! I don't know *what* they'd say if you
went to them with a perfectly good leg and
asked them to have it off.—And it's not the
sort of job you can do at home, is it?

MINNIE. No, indeed!

[*Pause.*]

GLADYS. But it's silly to be talking about cutting
legs off, now you've got a nice new one and
aren't ever going to have any trouble any more,
isn't it?

MINNIE [*her expression mixed perplexity and mis-*

giving]. Ah, indeed to gracious to goodness to glory whatever!

GLADYS. Isn't it funny, your not knowing how you got it? I didn't know people ever got legs suddenly like that. If it started as a little tiny wee one, and grew, that'd be quite scientific, wouldn't it? And no one *ever* bothers where scientific things come from, do they? But it *is* funny to get it all of a sudden. . . . I shouldn't worry, though, if I were you. After all, it's a jolly good leg, better than you'd expect, and that's the chief thing.

MINNIE. Is it, indeed? There's very *worried* I am, me having leg and—and—not knowing—where she coming from! [*On the brink of tears:*] I—not *liking* her at all, that's truth!

GLADYS. I think you're an ungrateful pig! It's trying to do its best for you, and then you go and be nasty to it! I don't suppose it likes doing housework a bit, but *it's* not complaining, is it? I think you're absolutely horrid to it!

MINNIE [*contritely*]. Ooo, leg bach, I am very sorry. Yes, indeed!

GLADYS. Anyhow, things always turn out for the best, don't they? There's a good and wise purpose behind everything that happens.

MINNIE. Well, yes, really . . . but you're the strange one to be saying that!

GLADYS. Yes, I know it sounds cynical of me . . .
but it's bitter experience! Oh, we know the odds
we're up against, don't you think we don't!
[*Ecstatically:*] It's *that* that makes the fight so
glorious, a few poor weak defenceless fiends
fighting against all the battalions of Heaven——

    [*A double knock at the door.*]

MINNIE. Well, to goodness, there's Scraggy Evan
the Post! Keep you quiet, leg bach; hide you
under my skirt, or there's awful lot of ex-
planations he'll be wanting! [*Goes to front
door.*]

SCRAGGY EVAN THE POST. Bore da, Mrs. Williams!
Sid'ych'i—Ooooooo!

    [MINNIE'S *leg refuses to be hidden, but
thrusts its ankle right under* EVAN'S *nose.*]

MINNIE. Bore da, Evan Post—quiet you, leg
bach!—There's no letters to go this morning—
Ooo, you shameless thing you, quiet!

EVAN. Well, indeed——

MINNIE. That's all, thank you fawr—— [*She
breaks down and runs for the bedroom stairs,
crying:*] Leg! Leg, you! [*It giving coquettish
little kicks into the air as she runs. Exit.* GLADYS
has hidden under the bed-clothes. SCRAGGY
EVAN *remains at the door for several seconds,
transfixed. Then pulls himself together, steps
in, and lays the post on the table. Exit, closing*

door. MR. WILLIAMS *comes heavily downstairs.*
GLADYS *snores a trifle exaggeratedly.*]

MR. WILLIAMS. Gladys! [*She snores.*] Gladys!—I
know you're not asleep, so don't pretend. [*She
makes a show of waking; yawns, stretches, and
catches sight of* MR. WILLIAMS.]

GLADYS. Oh, hallo! Good morning.

MR. WILLIAMS. Sit up: I want to talk to you.
    [*She does so, reluctantly.*]
What have you been doing to Mrs. Williams?

GLADYS. Me?

MR. WILLIAMS. Yes, you indeed.

GLADYS [*innocently*]. What should *I* have done to
her, Mr. Williams?

MR. WILLIAMS. She's crying. She ran upstairs at
a great speed, and there she is crying into her
pillow, the poor little girl.

GLADYS. But *I* haven't done anything, Mr.
Williams, really I haven't.

MR. WILLIAMS. Then why is she crying?

GLADYS. Have you asked her?

MR. WILLIAMS. Yes, indeed, but she won't
say.

GLADYS. If *she* won't tell you, *I* oughtn't to give
her away, ought I?

MR. WILLIAMS. Gladys! Gladys!

GLADYS. It wasn't me, I promise.

MR. WILLIAMS [*to himself*]. The question is becoming more and more uncertain as to whether I did right in exposing Minnie to danger as well as myself. But on the other hand, if it is right for me to face it, it is surely right for her also to face it. That would suggest that it is right for her to face it, and wrong for me to induce her to face it: in other words, it was wrong for me to induce her to do right. The question grows more and more complicated. [*To* GLADYS:] What have you done to her?

GLADYS. But Mr. Williams, *dear*, it wasn't me made her cry, really it wasn't.

MR. WILLIAMS. I don't see that there is any other possible conclusion.

GLADYS. I didn't.

MR. WILLIAMS. I am very much afraid that you are not speaking the truth.

GLADYS [*scandalized and indignant*]. Mr. Williams!

MR. WILLIAMS. Ah, dear me. But I suppose it would be inconsistent with her nature as a child of the Father of Lies to do anything else. But it is very distressing in such an innocent-looking little thing.

GLADYS. Mr. Williams! What will you say next? Of course I tell the truth, nearly always!

MR. WILLIAMS. Why, indeed?

GLADYS. Why? Oh, I don't know: it's the natural

thing to do, isn't it? I mean, you can do ever so
much more harm by telling the truth than you
ever could by lies, surely.

MR. WILLIAMS. Well, indeed!

GLADYS. We never break bargains, you know,
do we? That's one of our strong points.

MR. WILLIAMS. Your position is plausible, but I
hardly think it would prove tenable under
strict examination.

GLADYS. Oh, wouldn't it!—Mr. Williams, I do
wish you were on our side, you're much too
nice. [*Coaxingly:*] Mr. Williams, dear, what
are you so obstinate for? When you really see
the greatness and glory of evil, doesn't it stir
something within you? Don't you ever want
to fight against your old ways, and really
sincerely try to be bad?

MR. WILLIAMS [*in horror*]. You would have me
betray my cause?

GLADYS. No, no, not betray your cause, only
realize what your true cause is! Oh, Mr.
Williams, can't you *see* that the only thing in
life which matters is the glorious struggle
against the forces of good? To drive good
out of the world, and so at the Last Day to
receive the glorious crown of Victory! Can't
you *see* it? Everyone can help! Even a poor
little child like me can help: if only I could

win you to believe, I think I should be happy
for ever.

MR. WILLIAMS. The things you are saying,
Gladys, are very strange, very strange, and
they throw a great deal of light on a difficult
question. At first they filled me with horror,
but now I find them distinctly illuminating.
It has always been a mystery to me how a
mere negative such as the conception of evil
could have so much power in the world.
You have now convinced me that it is not a
mere negative, but that there are certain beings
to whom it presents at any rate the illusion of
a positive. Terrible though it be to admit it,
I see that your very existence is dependent
upon the conception of evil as a positive.
To wish you to be good would be to wish
your destruction: and at that point the argu-
ment becomes too difficult for me. Ah, me!—
Every day things grow more perplexing. And
there is poor little Minnie crying on her bed,
and I not able to discover the reason. I cannot
imagine what the creature can have done to
make her cry like that. I haven't seen her cry
like that, not ever, the poor dear thing.

GLADYS. I didn't do it, really I didn't! I wouldn't
hurt her, not for anything! *Dear* Mr. Williams,
really I wouldn't!

MR. WILLIAMS. Then what is the matter with her, you bad thing?

> [*By way of answer*, GLADYS *bursts into tears*.]

Gracious! Goodness! Don't you be crying too.

GLADYS [*through sobs*]. I didn't . . . it's horrid of you! . . . was *trying* to . . . won't believe me . . .

MR. WILLIAMS. The old bear I am! Gladys, child, Gladys!

> [*Enter* MINNIE.]

MINNIE. Ooo, what's the matter, 'nghariad? Oh, the poor little dear! [*Kneels beside to comfort her*.] Don't you cry, then, Gladys fach, merch-i!

GLADYS [*still sobbing*]. He said . . . he said . . . [*Suddenly flings her arms round* MINNIE'S *neck and kisses her*.]

MINNIE. There, the little top of an egg! Don't you cry, then! [GLADYS *grows calmer*.] That's right, dear; now run you upstairs and dress yourself! [GLADYS *gets out of bed—she is wearing one of* MINNIE'S *flannelette night-gowns, yards too big for her, and runs upstairs*.] Oh, the little bare feet on the cold stones! [*She begins folding up the bedding*.] What have you been saying to her, John Williams?

MR. WILLIAMS [*contritely*]. Ah, Minnie fach, there's the clumsy old bear I am! I didn't think!

MINNIE. Yes, indeed! You ought to be more gentle to her, John.—Oh, but she'll soon get over it, when she wash her face. She is a great comforting, the wash your face, isn't that so, really?

MR. WILLIAMS. Minnie, I am beginning to have grave doubts if I did right to undertake such terrible risks, on your account. Certainty, she is the Mother of Pride; and Pride she is the Old Aunt of Defeat.

MINNIE. Why are you always wonder was you doing right or was you wrong? The Love of Heaven, we having her if we do what we think to be right—she not expecting us to use better brains than she giving us, John; she not minding was it *really* right or wrong, not a snap of the fingers! It always comes right in the end, and you having faith, John. I not having good brains, but I standing just as good chances heaven like you, that's truth! And I having great deal more peace of mind into the bargain. [*Three slow laborious knocks at the door.*] Ai, gogoniant! There's some old fool at the door already! She knocking like Owain Flatfish, too! [*She retreats behind the table.*]

Open you the door, John bach, there's darling you are!

MR. WILLIAMS [*opening the door*]. Ah! Owain! How are you!

OWAIN FLATFISH [*trying to see round* MR. WILLIAMS; *talking English with extreme slowness and difficulty*]. Good day! Was you—want—little—piece—fishes?

MINNIE. What fishes have you, Owain?

OWAIN. Little—pieces—plaice. I having fresh—eels, very—good; having—haddutch!

MINNIE. Haven't you any trout to-day, then?

OWAIN. Well, no, really: [*brightens*] but perhaps I *finding* a nice piece trout, Mrs. Williams?

MINNIE. Oh, haven't you a rabbit, then?

OWAIN. Well, no, really; but perhaps [*looking at weather*] I *finding* nice fat rabbit, too. By—Thursday? She—do?—I have very nice pieces plaice, Mrs. Williams, they fresh—to-day. Look you, Mrs. Williams!

MINNIE [*refusing to come from behind table*]. Well, no, indeed; we not wanting anything to-day, thank you fawr, Owain!—Come and begin your breakfast, John.—Oh, shut the door, she blowing very cold!

[*He does so.*]

MR. WILLIAMS. Well, now, Minnie, where's our manners? Me shutting the door on Owain, and never offering him a cup of tea, indeed!—I'll call him.

MINNIE. Don't you do that, John.

MR. WILLIAMS. Why not, indeed?

MINNIE. Oh, someone else, p'r'aps they giving him tea! [*Bitterly.*] There's a great many visitors we shall be having to-day, John, believe me! Heaven knows what we doing with them all!

MR. WILLIAMS. Great many visitors! Why should we have that, girl fach?

MINNIE. Why? Oh, I don't know . . . but there *might* be a great many visitors coming this morning: you never know! [*Enter* GLADYS *and takes her place at the table.*] There's very full my cup is of strangers, yes, indeed!

MR. WILLIAMS. Nonsense, Minnie! That only means we want a new strainer in the pot.

MINNIE. P'r'aps so. . . . Or p'r'aps not so. . . . I only *thinking* there will be a great many people coming this morning . . . you never know.—You've been very quick, 'nghalon!

GLADYS. Yes: I never take long dressing.

MINNIE. Have you washed properly, girl? Behind your ears? [*Moves as if to look.*]

GLADYS [*fiercely*]. You leave my ears alone! Yes, I have!

MR. WILLIAMS. Gladys, Gladys! You mustn't speak to Mrs. Williams like that!

GLADYS. I'm sorry, but I can't stand people messing about with my ears.

MINNIE. Well, yes, indeed: I was forgetting about her ears, John.—Was you wash your teeth?

GLADYS. Yes.

MINNIE. That's good. Will you have some more tea?

GLADYS. Thank you, Mrs. Williams.

MINNIE. No?

GLADYS. Yes, please.

MINNIE [*referring to the bread and butter*]. Oh, well, she's not so stale as she might be, John: I covering her over with a plate.

MR. WILLIAMS [*dramatically*]. To goodness, Minnie, there's me was forgetting all about it!

MINNIE. Forgetting what, then?

MR. WILLIAMS. I ought to go and see Mrs. Twin Jones. She's very ill indeed, the poor little girl.

MINNIE. Well, yes, the dear little girl; and she used to having twins or even triplets ever since she was married, and now it's only one. It was a great shock to her, really. There's awful bad she is, they saying. But don't you be very long, John; don't you forget they ironing!

G

MR. WILLIAMS. Mightn't I do the ironing to-morrow, perhaps?

MINNIE. Well, no, indeed; I seeing the gentleman from The Royal Goat yesterday, awful dirty the collar she wearing, the poor thing: I think she not having any more.—Wouldn't I do it for you, John?

MR. WILLIAMS. No, indeed! You lifting a heavy iron, indeed! There's careful you must be of your heart, Minnie!—I won't be long. Ah, dear me! [*Gets up and prepares to go.*] Well, now, where's my hat?

MINNIE. They upstairs! I putting them out of the dust. [*Exit* MINNIE, *stairs.*]

MR. WILLIAMS. Be a good girl, Gladys dear.

GLADYS [*laughing*]. Oh, I expect I *shall* be! It is fun being on a job where you can let yourself rip, and be thoroughly good for a bit. But it's going to be an awful strain: getting back to proper wickedness, I mean. Giving in and being good is so easy.

MR. WILLIAMS [*to himself*]. Well, indeed, what shall I be saying to poor Mrs. Twin?

GLADYS [*coming up to him and taking his hand*]. I do love you both so, Mr. Williams. Won't you kiss me?

MR. WILLIAMS [*disapprovingly*]. Well, indeed, you little silly. Be you a good girl, and help Mrs.

Williams about the house! That's better than kissing!

[GLADYS *makes a face. Enter* MINNIE.]

MINNIE. Here's your hat, John bach.

MR. WILLIAMS. Thank you! Thank you! Good-bye, my dear. [*Kisses* MINNIE; *turns to go.*]

GLADYS [*in a small piteous voice*]. John bach! Good-bye, John bach!

MINNIE. Well, I never! You cheeky little thing, you! I never heard! Go upstairs at once, you naughty little thing! [GLADYS *half rises.*] Go on!

MR. WILLIAMS. Ah, she didn't mean anything, Minnie.

MINNIE. We can't letting her be cheeky, John, or there's no knowing where it would end!—Go on upstairs at once, you! [*Exit* GLADYS.] I never heard, no, indeed! Good gracious me!

[MR. WILLIAMS *moves towards the door again.*]

MARI BAKEHOUSE [*off*]. Mrs. Williams?

MINNIE. Goodness me!—come you in, Mari dear!

[*Enter* MARI.]

MR. WILLIAMS. Good day, Mari. I am sorry that I have to be going out, so I will leave you to talk with Mrs. Williams. [*Exit.*]

MINNIE. Come and have a cup of tea, sit you down, sit you down.

MARI. No, thank you fawr, Mrs. Williams, I just taking tea.

MINNIE. Well to goodness, take you another, then!

MARI. No, thank you, really! [MINNIE *gives her a cup*.] Well, thank you very much.

MINNIE. Was you—seeing—Evan the Post this morning, Mari?

MARI. Well, no, indeed; there wasn't any letters this morning.

MINNIE. Was you—hearing any news in the village this morning, then?

MARI. Well, no, indeed; I came straight up. Is there any news, then?

MINNIE. Well, yes. . . . I having a new leg.

MARI. Well, indeed, that's good. He was getting awfully worn at the end, the old one. But they're awful expensive, the legs, isn't that so?

MINNIE. Well, yes, really.

MARI. And who was making her? Not John Joiner?

MINNIE. No, she was not John Joiner.

MARI. She's not that beautiful leg with brass round it, that was in the catalogue from Liverpool, is she?

MINNIE. No, it was not Liverpool she coming from.

MARI. Ah, that was the grand, handsome leg!

But may I see her, Mrs. Williams? Are you wearing her, then?

MINNIE [*dramatically*]. Well, I *am* wearing her, then, and I think I shall wear her for ever and ever, and ever and ever, God forgive me!— Look you!

MARI. Oh! But she is beautiful! She's pretty as a picture, yes, indeed! Just like real! Well, I never! Ah, indeed! Well, well! Goodness gracious!—And does she fit comfortable, then?

MINNIE. She fitting *perfectly*!

MARI. Duw anwyl! Well, indeed!—Let me see you walk, then! [MINNIE *does so.*] Oh, it is lovely! But where did you get her, then?

MINNIE [*awkwardly*]. Well, now, that's very strange; but I can't tell you.

MARI. A present, like?

MINNIE. Well, yes.

GLADYS [*on stairs*]. May I come down yet, Mrs. Williams?—I'm sorry!

MINNIE. Very well, then, come you!

[*Enter* GLADYS.]

Go and say good morning to Miss Jones, Gladys.

GLADYS. How do you do?

MARI. I'm very well, thank you!—Well, there's a

great many surprises you've got for us this morning, Mrs. Williams! I didn't know you had anyone stopping!

GLADYS. I only came last night.

MARI. Well, that's nice, really! How do you like it here?

GLADYS. Very much indeed.

MARI. Well, yes, it's very nice in summer.

GLADYS. Oh, Miss Jones, what a lovely brooch!

MARI. You like it?

MINNIE. Is that the one Timothy brought you from Blackpool, Mari?

MARI. Well, yes.

GLADYS. I think it's lovely!

MARI. Oh, it's not so bad, truly.

GLADYS. And don't you like Mrs. Williams' leg? Isn't *that* lovely?

MARI. It was beautiful! I was asking her where it come from, but she won't say. P'r'aps she thinking we all going to cut off our legs, so as to buy nice ones like that! [*Laughing.*]

GLADYS [*in astonishment*]. But, Miss Jones . . .

MARI. Well?

GLADYS. Surely you know it's *real*?

MARI. Oh, the little dear! [*Laughing.*] The darling! Well, if that isn't simple!

GLADYS. But it *is* real!

MINNIE [*quickly*]. How is your Grannie's rheumatism, then, Mari? [*Aside to* GLADYS:] Quiet, you little silly! Don't tell such wicked fibs!

GLADYS [*loudly*]. I'm not telling fibs! Of course it's real.—Look! [*Against* MINNIE'S *will the leg begins to show itself rather fully from under her skirt*.]

MARI. Well, I never! It's not surprising you took it for real, no, indeed!

GLADYS. But you *feel* it!

MINNIE. Will you be quiet, you wicked little thing! Tell such *stories*, indeed!

GLADYS. Touch it!

MARI. Well, I'll touch it if you like.

MINNIE [*quickly*]. They padding her, they making her soft, *just* like real!

MARI [*running her fingers over the calf*]. Well, I never! Just like, you couldn't hardly tell! [*Suddenly:*] It's *warm*! There's *bones*! Duw anwyl! [*Starts back*.] Tell me the truth, Mrs. Williams is she . . . ? [MINNIE *bursts into tears*.] She is! Oh, good gracious! It's a miracle! Glory be!

MINNIE [*still angry*]. Gladys, you *wicked* little thing——

GLADYS. But it's only the *truth* I was telling, Mrs. Williams——

MARI. Why shouldn't she say, the darling? It's all very well to be humble, but when there's a

real miracle done to you, surely it isn't grateful
to be keeping it dark, Mrs. Williams!

MINNIE. You *wouldn't* have believed me . . .
and now you don't believe me either!

MARI. Mrs. Williams, I am *that* glad! [*Flings her
arms round her and kisses her.*] But how did it
come? Was it just praying, like? Or was it for
something special?

GLADYS. She was very kind to *me*, you know,
Miss Jones. I hurt myself in the road last
night, and she took me in and nursed me just
as if I was her own little girl. She thoroughly
deserves it.

MARI. Well, I'm sure she does, the darling! So
that's it!—But aren't you proud to have a
miracle happen on your account, and you just
an ordinary little girl?

GLADYS. Me? Oh, yes, of course I'm frightfully
bucked.

MARI. Well, I should think so, indeed! There's
no wonder you were telling!

MINNIE. Mari Bakehouse, dear——

MARI. Well, then?

MINNIE. Will you promise me, you not saying
anything?

MARI. No, indeed! Why shouldn't I? If you're so
humble, there's no reason we shouldn't be
giving glory to God!—Well, now, isn't it

wonderful to think of a miracle happening
Church, and all these years they only happening Chapel!—I'm thinking I'm not sorry
Timothy has turned Church, though it was a
great disgrace I thought it before!

MINNIE. Oh, Mari fach——

MARI. No, indeed! I'll run straight down and tell
my Granny. She would be very angry with me
if she wasn't the first to know.

MINNIE. Scraggy Evan the Post, he knows.

MARI. Oh, twt, twt! He'll be telling everyone
before I get outside!—But he doesn't know
everything! He hasn't *felt* it, has he, Mrs.
Williams?

MINNIE. Well, no, indeed!

MARI. Ah, that's good! Now I must run quick!
Glory, glory, glory, glory, glory! [*Exit.*]

MINNIE [*slowly*]. Well, you: there's a pretty mess
things *you* making!

GLADYS. Me?

MINNIE. Yes, you indeed! Why couldn't you keep
your little tongue in his place?

GLADYS. But, Mrs. Williams, I only told the
truth.

MINNIE. Only told the truth, indeed! And
is it the truth she's believing? Tell me
that!

GLADYS. Well, practically.

MINNIE. Practically! What does *practically* the truth mean? Awful lies, I'm thinking! Me, being the sort to have a miracle done to me by Heaven.—If it had been John, now, that was different, the great saint he is! But me! And now they'll be making a great fuss over me, same as they made over Mrs. Resurrection Jones, when she tap inside her coffin at her own funeral, and they let her out. And me not deserving! There's all hollow I shall feel, me the great uncommon lying whitened sepulchre! [*Crying again:*] I don't know what to do, indeed I don't! Oh, John, why he not coming back?

GLADYS. Mrs. Williams, dear! [MINNIE *goes over to mantelpiece.* GLADYS *puts her arm round her to comfort her. The door opens and* OWAIN FLATFISH *advances silently and mysteriously into the room.*] But they may be right! You never know! After all, you don't really *know* where that leg came from, do you? Isn't it just as likely to be a miracle as any other way? [*She creeps away from* MINNIE; *fixes* OWAIN *with her eye. For several seconds they stand facing each other, immobile. Then* GLADYS *makes a sudden pass with her hand:* OWAIN, *in a slightly bent position, with no change of expression whatever, suddenly shoots out of the door again backwards on a wire.*

GLADYS *wipes her brow and slips back to* MINNIE.]
There's no reason why Heaven *shouldn't* have
done it, is there? Heaven does an awful lot no
one ever suspects it of, you know.

MINNIE. Oh, she wicked, wicked leg; she going to
give me nothing but vexation, I know that!

GLADYS. Mother dear! Don't cry! It will all
come right in the end, I know it will!

MINNIE [*affectionately*]. There's a little comforter
you are, girl fach! Well, well; tears, they not
do any good.

[*The door bursts open. Enter* MARI *and*
MRS. JONES BAKEHOUSE *behind her.*]

Well, this is nice to see you, Mrs. Jones
Bakehouse, yes, indeed.

MARI [*excitedly*]. Go and pinch it, Grannie!

MRS. JONES BAKEHOUSE. I am sorry to call so
early, Mrs. Williams, but I am catching the
motor for Ynysllanbedrbachdeudraethgerylan,
and I thought perhaps I could do a little
shopping for you?

MINNIE [*awkwardly*]. Well, that's very kind, yes,
indeed——

MRS. JONES [*coughing*]. Oh, dear, there's a smell of
sulphur very strong somewhere.

MINNIE. Well, yes, indeed, it's they plaguy wasps!
Mr. Williams, she just smoke out one nest, and
here are they worse nor ever.

MRS. JONES. Wasp-nests so late as this? Well, that's strange!

MINNIE. I did not say wasps. It was the wall-paper.

MRS. JONES. Wall-paper?

MINNIE. The doctor saying the scarlet fever, p'r'aps she hiding behind the wall-paper. So was we fumigate the whole house, yes, indeed.

MRS. JONES. Well, indeed——

MINNIE. Well, you're very kind, Mrs. Jones, but I don't think of anything we wanting at Ynys to-day, thank you fawr.

MRS. JONES. No?

MINNIE. No, indeed, thank you.

MRS. JONES. And this is the little stranger?

MINNIE. Well, yes.

GLADYS. Isn't her leg fine?

MARI. Go and feel it, Grannie! It's warm!

MRS. JONES. Twt, twt!—You must come and have tea with Mari and me one day.

GLADYS. Thank you, that would be nice.

MINNIE [*desperately*]. Mrs. Jones!

MRS. JONES. Well, indeed?

MINNIE. Was Mari telling you about my leg?

MRS. JONES. Well, she did say something casually——

MINNIE. It's true.

MRS. JONES [*quite unmoved*]. Indeed? I am very glad.

MINNIE. Look you!

MRS. JONES. Well, yes, it is very fine.

MINNIE. It is a strange thing to be happening to a quiet, respectable person.

MRS. JONES [*ironically*]. Indeed, yes, very strange. —But if you're sure there's no shopping you want, I won't keep you!

MINNIE. Oh, but I'm glad to see you—stop you a little.

MRS. JONES [*coldly*]. Well, thank you, but I had better be going back. [*Exit*, MARI *after her*.]

MINNIE. Well, she behaving very strange.

GLADYS. Didn't she?

MINNIE. I wonder who will be coming next. This is a very terrible morning, that's truth.

[MARI *bursts in*.]

MARI. Mrs. Williams!

MINNIE. Well?

MARI. She doesn't believe it!

MINNIE. No?

MARI. She says the shops in London are full of legs like that, in the windows, with silk stockings on them and electric lights!

MINNIE. Well, the unbelieving Turk! I didn't

think it of her!—But what can you expect of
an Albanian Baptist! I always said that sect
was the worst of the lot!

GLADYS. What a beast!

MARI. And she told me not to tell you!

MINNIE. Oh, the serpent! She, going to corrupt
the village against me! And I, thinking she was
a good friend, really!

MARI. She is a very knowing one, Grannie. . . .
Mrs. Williams, why did you tell me it was a
miracle, if it was really an artificial one, then?
It wasn't nice of you, at all, then.

MINNIE. Me, saying she real?

MARI. I didn't think it of you.

GLADYS. Don't be silly, of course it's real.

MARI. And deceiving the poor child, too,
Grannie says.

MINNIE. Well, I never!

MARI. Yes, indeed.

MINNIE. Mari Bakehouse, *dear*!

GLADYS. Didn't you feel it?

MARI. Well, yes, it felt real; but, Grannie, she's
the knowing one.

GLADYS. You don't seem to have much faith, for
all you're a Baptist, Miss Jones; feeling it
and *then* not believing.

MARI [*bewildered*]. Why, are you saying really
. . . ?

GLADYS. Your Grannie didn't feel it, did she? I've seen those legs in London; they look very nice, but they're made of pink china. They're *hard*.

MARI. What a wicked sinner I am, that's true: I'm a disgrace to my religion! Why, if I was a proper religious one, I'd believe everything was a miracle unless it was proved to me not, like the old minister at Pandy and the frog's eggs in his kettle! And now me having no faith over a little thing like a leg! But it is strange for a miracle to happen Church, all the same! —And it's very strange for Grannie to be wrong, that too!

MINNIE. I am afraid your Grannie she very worldly woman, Mari granddaughter Bake-house!

GLADYS. Anyhow, it *must* be a miracle because she deserves one.

MARI. Well, that's logical anyway: you can't get over that.

GLADYS [*to* MINNIE]. Why not kill her?

MINNIE. Kill who?

GLADYS. Mrs. Jones.

MINNIE. Gladys!

GLADYS. Before she goes spreading her nasty atheistical views about. As a warning.

MINNIE. You wicked——

GLADYS. I'm not! The prophets did it, didn't they? And what's good enough for a prophet to do is good enough for anyone, surely. Why not make a bear eat her?

MARI. Make a bear eat my poor old Grannie?

MINNIE. And after she offering to do my shopping in Ynys for me?

GLADYS. But if it's a case of Duty, you oughtn't to let personal reason stand in your way. You could, you know: if you could grow a leg like that in a night, you could surely make a bear eat Mrs. Jones. Think of the effect it would have in the village!

MINNIE. It would have a great uncommon effect, that's true. Mrs. Jones Bakehouse, she meeting Mrs. Evans Boots. "Have you heard?" she says, and Mrs. Boots: "No, indeed; what is it, then?" "Well, there's out of the world you are, you not hearing the news." "But what is the news?" And Mrs. Jones, she saying: "Mrs. Williams, wife of Church, she buying a china leg and pretending it a miracle." And Mrs. Boots: "Well, and is it not a miracle really?" And Mrs. Jones, she say: "No, indeed," and what is coming down the road? A great black bear, as big as a horse, with flames in his mouth, and his eyes like lamps motor-bicycle, and he eating Mrs. Jones without saying a word. That would make a great sensation; yes, really, glory be.

GLADYS. And if that doesn't convert Mrs. Boots, I don't know what would.

MINNIE. Well, yes, indeed, it would be a good thing for Mrs. Boots' soul, and that's truth!

MARI. But, Mrs. Williams, you won't let it eat my Grannie?

MINNIE. Well, no, indeed, Mari. I was only *suppose*. . . . It would be a great, redeeming miracle, that. But I not doing it really. I was only suppose. . . . And there's the bear rattling a chain of fire round his neck, and leaving footprints in the road big as a duck pond. And Mrs. Jones, she saying: "I don't *believe* in her old leg," and the bear he swallowing her with the wicked words in her mouth. And Mrs. Boots, she falling on her knees, she singing Hallelujah, and—— But I not doing it really, Mari Jones. I only suppose.

MARI. I don't hardly like to speak to you, Mrs. Williams, and you doing such things to my Grannie.

MINNIE. But I only *suppose*, Mari dear: I wouldn't hurt her little finger, not *really*.

GLADYS. Well, if you won't kill her, why not cure her rheumatism?

MINNIE. Well, yes, indeed, that's better! She

H

coming to the house, and she saying it's china. And I say: "Touch it!" And she saying: "No, indeed." And I saying: "Touch it!" And she touching it, and her rheumatism she fly away. There's pretty she would be, the miracle bach!—But I *would* like to see a great black bear, big as a mountain, and the flames coming out of his ears, and he eating her up all of a sudden, and she an Albanian Baptist!

GLADYS. But perhaps it would be kinder to cure her rheumatism. Why not do it really instead of just supposing?

MINNIE [*scandalized*]. Me *really* make her good? Was you say that earnest?

GLADYS. Why not?

MINNIE. Do you suppose I not having any more real religion than that! Me, doing miracles, as I fancy, out of sport!

MARI. But why not make her well? What harm is there in that?

MINNIE. And how would I be doing it, then, Mari Bakehouse?

MARI. Oh, I don't know. Praying, perhaps?

MINNIE. It's not by praying I'd do it, indeed; or it's a queer wicked sort of praying it would be!

GLADYS. But wasn't it by praying you got your leg?

MINNIE. Gladys!

GLADYS. But *didn't* you pray for one?

MINNIE [*slowly*]. I didn't think it was in *this* world I would be answered. I not expecting all this trouble is on me—me, a poor quiet sinner; it isn't fair, that's truth, indeed! My head she not clever, and I not having any education, I only trying do what my conscience telling me; and now my old conscience she going round in my head like a wheel, till I don't know God from the Devil.

MARI. But what's the matter?

MINNIE. My conscience, she *was* saying, Minnie Williams, do this, and I doing it; or do that, and I doing it; but now she saying: "What ought you to do, Minnie Williams?" And I saying: "Don't ask me that, my old conscience, it's yòu was ought to saying." And then she saying nothing at all, and |I am so down-hearted I think I shall die.

GLADYS. Poor Mrs. Williams!

MINNIE. Gladys fach, there's more trouble I am having of your coming to me than if you was my own child.

GLADYS. It isn't all my fault really. [*Goes to her.*]

MINNIE [*drawing back*]. To think you was *that*, and looking so!

GLADYS [*drawing back too*]. Yes, I am, and that's

why! *I* never doubt! I know what to do, and I do it! I serve my master faithfully, and shall do for ever and ever: it's the only thing I live for, and I love it and glory in it! *He* never leaves me wondering what to do; it's all so simple, and so peaceful; once you give your heart to it, there's never any more doubt . . . Mother dear . . .

MINNIE [*trembling*]. I think I shall kill you!

GLADYS. . . . Won't you just try it?

MARI [*awkwardly*]. Well, what queer way are you two going on?

[MINNIE *crosses to shelf where Bible is*.]

GLADYS [*in cold, hard voice*]. Kindly remember we're not alone.

MARI. Good gracious me, what is the trouble?

[*A rat-tat on the window-pane: it is* TIMOTHY.]

[*In loud whisper:*] Where's your manners, Tim? Knock you at the door, proper! [*He does so and enters.* MINNIE *sits wearily on music stool;* GLADYS *is once more all smiles, and directs her attention to* TIMOTHY.]

TIMOTHY YSGAIRNOLWEN. Good day, Mrs. Williams!—Mari, I met your Grannie and she said you were up here. [*In low voice:*] Say, what's all this hanky-panky about Minnie Williams' leg?

MARI. Sht!

GLADYS. Was it you gave Miss Jones that lovely brooch?

[MINNIE *crosses the stage to put the table between herself and* TIMOTHY; *sits down, staring in front of her despondently.*]

TIMOTHY. Natty little piece, isn't it? I know a bit of jewelry when I see it: best rolled gold, that is!—Who is the young lady, Mari? Won't you introduce us, or are you jealous?

MARI. Sht! Don't go putting ideas into the child's head.

TIMOTHY. She'll get them herself soon enough, don't you worry!

GLADYS. My name is Gladys; I'm staying with Mrs. Williams.

TIMOTHY. Chin, chin, kid! [*aside to* MARI:] But I say, old girl, what *is* this leg business?—She doesn't look up to much, is the old lady ill? [*Aloud.*] I hope you'll pardon my dropping in like this, Mrs. Williams.

MINNIE. You're welcome.

[OWAIN FLATFISH'S *face is visible at the window a moment.*]

GLADYS [*in terror*]. Oh, *who's* that horrid man?

TIMOTHY [*opening door*]. Cerr'o'ffor', hen crwydryn!—He's gone; I can't see a sign of

him. Wicked old blighter, frightening the
kid like that!

GLADYS [*quickly*]. No, he's not *wicked*!

TIMOTHY [*taking no notice*]. Here's old Gas Jones
coming up the street, though. Grannie's with
him, Mari. D'you think they're coming here?
—Oh, look you, Grannie's carrying on like a
two-year-old!

[MARI *joins him at the door*.]

MINNIE. Make them go away!

GLADYS. Why?

MINNIE. I hate them, I, I—— *Please*.

GLADYS [*going over to her*]. Mummie dear, it'll be
all right after this morning. Once they're used
to it, they'll forget about it. Do face it out just
for now!

MR. GAS JONES [*off*]. Good morning, Timothy.
This *is* a surprise!

TIMOTHY. Good day, Gas.

MARI. Good day, Mr. Jones. [*All four talk together
rapidly in Welsh*.]

MINNIE. Please!

GLADYS. Poor Mummie! You do look tired.
But I promise you it'll go all right with me
here: I know how to manage them.

MINNIE. But why not make them go away, you?

GLADYS. I can't: there are some things I have to
do, for conscience, don't you see? Like you

have to do what is right in big things, but in little things it doesn't matter doing what is kind and nice? It's the same with me. They've got to come, but I promise I'll see it goes all right. I promise I'll make them be nice to you.

MINNIE. I wish I knowing what you was doing next, you!

GLADYS [*with change of manner*]. *Me!* But it's none of *my* doing: the Postman must have told them.

MINNIE [*rising*]. Come in, Mr. Jones. [*Enter* MR. GAS JONES.] Come in, Mrs. Jones Bakehouse.

[*Enter* MRS. JONES BAKEHOUSE.]

MR. GAS JONES [*in gentlemanly astonishment*]. Well, good gracious me! I never expected— why, you've quite a party this morning, Mrs. Williams! I just happened to be passing, and saw Timothy at the door——

GLADYS. Oh, Mrs. Jones! I *am* glad to see you again! I had a horrid fear something might have happened to you.

MRS. JONES [*stiffly*]. Indeed? And what, pray?

GLADYS. Oh, I don't know . . . just something.

MR. GAS JONES. There now! Isn't that just what I was saying? Isn't that the very way rumours get started? We shall be being told next that Mrs. Jones has been murdered, good gracious me!

MRS. JONES. I shouldn't have much difficulty in disproving *that* charge, Mr. Jones.

MR. GAS JONES. Well, no, on the evidence we hold you acquitted, Mrs. Jones! [*Laughs exaggeratedly.*] But it certainly is strange, the *ridiculous* stories that do get about sometimes, isn't it, friends? [*Everyone stirs uneasily.*] Now, there's that story—you'd hardly believe me—it really is too *ridiculous*—but you can't think what story—it really is *frightfully* funny —Evan Post has got hold of to-day!—He must be quite mad, I suppose. It's so fantastical. I really must laugh——

[*Enter* MRS. RESURRECTION JONES, *out of breath.*]

MRS. RESURRECTION JONES [*majestically*]. Good day, all! [*Immediate hush.*]

MR. GAS JONES. Why, if it isn't Mrs Resurrection——

MRS. RES. JONES. Good day, Mrs. Williams!

MINNIE [*faintly*]. Good day.

MRS. RES. JONES. The Lord has treated me with most *especial* mercies; but I am told that on you also the cup of His balm has overflowed. Let me see it. Praised be the Name of the Lord! [MR. GAS JONES *effaces himself and looks out of the window.* TIMOTHY *does not.* MINNIE *walks out from behind table, displaying her foot and ankle*. MRS. RESURRECTION *comes up to her, goes down on her knees to examine it. In a tone of bitterest disappointment:*] Praised be the Lord, it's true! [*She rises and marches straight out of the house, slamming the door behind her.*]

MR. GAS JONES [*reappearing*]. We were just discussing the question of rumours. Would you believe it, I heard the most laughable story about the Ellises of Arno!

MRS. JONES. Remember they are cousins of mine, Mr. Jones!

MR. GAS JONES. Well, indeed! But I expect everyone *claims* to be a cousin of yours, Mrs. Jones.

MARI.	Poor Mrs. Resurrection!
GLADYS	[*pensively*]. It must be rather fun being the local miracle.
TIMOTHY	[*suddenly, with great conviction*]. Well, this is a rum business! I don't like it all!—Mari!

[All at once.]

MARI. Yes?

TIMOTHY. Let's get out of this. I can't stick this sort of business! It isn't square!

[*He moves towards the door, but before he can get there* MR. GAS JONES *has cleared his throat and begun to speak.*]

MR. GAS JONES. I hope I shall not be committing any breach of good taste in referring to the incident which we have just—which has just taken place. Ladies and gentlemen, it has frequently been my pleasant task to say a few informal words of congratulation to my friends, whether upon the merit of some personal achievement or upon some particular piece of good fortune. But never before, I think you will admit, never before have we been present on a precisely similar occasion; indeed, for such an occasion it is difficult to find suitable words in which to express our sentiments.

[GLADYS *suddenly screams and runs to* MRS. WILLIAMS.]

GLADYS. Oh, save me, save me!

MINNIE. What is it?

GLADYS. Oh, don't leave me, hold me tight!

MINNIE. What's the matter, then?

GLADYS. Oh, save me, I'm so frightened.

MINNIE. But what is it, then, you silly?

GLADYS. Oh, it's going wrong, something dreadful is going to happen in a minute, I know!

MINNIE. There's nothing to hurt you, then; what's the trouble?

MARI [*flinging her arms around her*]. Gladys darling, there's nothing to hurt you!

GLADYS. I don't know . . . I'm better now . . . no, I'm silly, that's all.

MRS. JONES. That child wants a good hard slap!

[*Enter suddenly* OWAIN FLATFISH *with bell,
book and candle; passes through the astonished
crowd, driving* GLADYS *before him, right to
the door:* GLADYS *looking very white and
trying hard not to cry; he chanting the while:*]
OWAIN.

> In Nomine Nominum
> Quæ cantantur apud Dominum
> Salvatorem omnium hominum
> > Coniuro te!
> Per mundi Lucem
> Veram Crucem
> > Coniuro te!
> Per angelorum sanctitatem,
> Per libri huius potestatem
> Ut abeas
> Ad inferas
> > Coniuro te!
> Filia diabolorum
> Et serpentum maculatorum
> A domibus sanctissimorum
> A conspectu sancto horum
> In regiones damnatorum
> In sæcula sæculorum
> > Nunc discede
> > Celeri pede
> > > Coniuro te!

GLADYS [*drawing herself up in the doorway*]. Bully!
    [GLADYS *disappears, and* OWAIN *passes out
after her.*]

MINNIE. *[All at once.]* Gladys! Gladys! [*Bursting into tears.*]

MRS. J. B. Amen to all that, whatever it was.

MR. G. J. Well, good gracious me! Who would have thought!

TIMOTHY. I say, Gas, Owain's mad! He'll frighten the poor kid out of her wits!

MARI. Run you and save her, Tim, quick!

MR. GAS JONES. It is best not to interfere.

MARI. Coward!

MR. GAS JONES. My dear, there's something here I don't understand. There is something that tells me that if I interfere I shall make a mess of things. If it was an earthly battle, I would be much tempted to interfere on behalf of the weaker. But I detect in this, as in so much that has happened to-day, an element—do not laugh at me, I am absolutely serious—of the supernatural. The ways of God are inscrutable, and it is not for man to put his foot in them.

TIMOTHY. To hell with the supernatural! That child's being frightened by that old—— [*Exit.*]

MARI. Oh Timw bach, don't go, you'll get hurt——

[MR. GAS JONES *suddenly swears and goes to run after him;* MRS. JONES *blocks the way.*]

MRS. JONES. It's all very well for young men to be fools, Gas, but you know well enough there's something here mortal man had best keep out of!

MR. GAS JONES. But it seems so . . . there seems something so awfully *mean* in letting a child be treated——

MRS. JONES. If it was risking your life, that's one thing; but risking your immortal soul's another altogether. It's a worse risk, and there's no merit in it either.

MARI [*stupidly*]. But what was it, Grannie? Was that the devil disguised as Owain Dwl?

MRS. JONES. I'm not going to discuss it with you, child; I don't know what it means, or who's what, and the less we talk, the better, I'm thinking. That's no common child, and I'm not sorry she's gone.

MARI. Do you remember the stories you used to tell me, Grannie, about the Little People, and they changing children?

MR. GAS JONES. Mari, I'm sorry you're so superstitious as to speak of fairies, which are not even Christian! Angels and devils there are, and *they're* religious, but fairies, without any moral sense at all either for right *or* wrong—I'm ashamed to hear you mention such things! I'm sorry you should encourage her, Mrs.

Jones! You know very well the Chapel doesn't
hold with fairies!

MRS. JONES. Twt, man, you can't be always reading a child the book of Deuteronomy! There's
no harm in telling them a tale or two if it's a
good one.

[*Re-enter* TIMOTHY.]

MARI. Tim! what happened?

TIMOTHY. Nothing.

MARI. Didn't you see them?

TIMOTHY. No.

MARI. What did you see, then?

TIMOTHY. Nothing at all.

MARI [*disappointed*]. Oh, Timw! I did think you'd
see *something*.

TIMOTHY. Well, not much.

MARI. What was it?

TIMOTHY. Well, I didn't exactly *see* anything;
but it was awfully queer.

MARI. What was queer?

TIMOTHY. Oh, I don't know; just everything.

MRS. JONES. Mari, stop asking about what
doesn't concern you. And you, Timothy, I
hope you're properly ashamed of yourself for
interfering.

TIMOTHY [*slowly*]. I guess, Mrs. Jones, if there's
anyone to question about this business, it's
Mrs. Williams!

MR. GAS JONES. Mrs Williams is overcome by her feelings, Timothy. We should certainly do better to wait for a more auspicious moment before troubling her with our foolish questions: when I have no doubt, no doubt at all, that she will answer us, that she will give us a thoroughly satisfactory explanation. I am sure that whatever part she has taken in the matter is a most highly creditable one. I have every confidence in Mrs. Williams. I am sure you will all agree with me. I am sure that this leg, which she undoubtedly possesses, has come to her in a manner altogether open and above-board, in a manner redounding purely to her credit. If it seems to us that she has been keeping very doubtful company, company about whom some unexplained mystery exists: if we find her showing apparent grief at the loss of that company: if we find her possessed of a limb of apparently doubtful source, and (if we are to believe Evan Post) more than question-able tendencies: in short, if apparently there is much in this matter for regret, much to pray Heaven for forgiveness for, with tears, fasting, and sincere pentitence, I am sure the fault lies with *us*, that Mrs. Williams is in no way to blame, that by some simple explanation she will put all our unworthy doubts at rest.

MARI. Mrs. Williams, who *was* Gladys?

MRS. JONES. Why isn't your leg clothed more godly, instead of in that foreign stuff?

TIMOTHY. Mrs. Williams, what sort of a game have you been trying to play on us? Because we're not going to stand it, do you see?

MARI. I wonder *you* dare to speak, Timothy son of Ysgairnolwen, after disgracing yourself by interfering with the Act of God!

MR. GAS JONES. Don't trouble her, the poor thing: she will answer us all in good time; there is no hurry whatever to reply, Mrs. Williams.

MARI. Who was she? Oh, I *knew* there was something wrong about her the moment I saw her! Yes, really I did!

[MINNIE *rises, backs down stage, struggling with her leg*.]

MINNIE. Leg, leg, you old fool, if you kick her I'll never forgive you!

MR. GAS JONES [*hurriedly*]. Calm yourself, Mrs. Williams!—Friends, I think our most graceful action would be to retire, retire immediately.

[MR. WILLIAMS *has entered unobserved, and comes down stage*.]

MR. WILLIAMS. Well, good gracious me, what a lot of visitors you have, Minnie!

MR. GAS JONES. We had called, Mr. Williams, to

tender our congratulations to Mrs. Williams upon her new leg.

MR. WILLIAMS. New leg . . . well, bless me, what an old blind mole I am! I had never noticed!

CURTAIN

I

ACT III

SCENE: *The same, a year later. To denote the lapse of time,* MINNIE'S *silk stocking is full of ladders and darned with wool, the heel of the shoe almost worn away. It is early afternoon, but the blind is down.*

Everyone is in black. MINNIE *is lying in the big chair.* MRS. JONES BAKEHOUSE *is doing a little washing up in a corner.* MARI BAKEHOUSE *is sobbing unrestrainedly.* TIMOTHY *is standing by her.* GAS *moves about a good deal, deftly, in silence.*

MARI. When I was little he always gave me peppermints, always.

TIMOTHY. He caught me stealing his apples once, out of the rectory garden. Coo, I was scared. He nabbed me by the arm and said he wondered if he ought to go and tell the man they belonged to. I didn't see the joke then, I was only a kid! But I do now.

MARI. Did he let you go?

TIMOTHY. Sure. He went off talking to himself, about it being his duty to tell the owner if he could find him. But I wasn't half scared.

MRS. JONES. I think it's often we didn't understand all he meant, any of us.

MARI. I *never* understood him, not *ever*, and now I shan't get another chance to! But it was beautiful, the things he said.

TIMOTHY. He was a good sport, you can't get over that!

MRS. JONES. I'm an old woman, I never thought to live to see *his* burying. I never thought, a year ago, of me and Gas getting married. It's strange, the things which happen you'd never have thought of.

MR. GAS JONES. Well, yes: life is made up of the unexpected.

MRS. JONES. He was a great saint: I've never seen such another.

MR. GAS JONES. He was indeed; and moreover he was a man of the highest intellectual ability.

MARI. Why, surely: he was a B.A., B.D.

MR. GAS JONES. If you won't misunderstand me, I would almost say he was a poet.

MARI. I remember the way he used to smile on us, passing in the street. We was all fond of him, yes, truly!

MRS. JONES. We often had a joke together, he and I, about the young folks.

MR. GAS JONES. Everybody on the Parish Council looked up to him in the most extraordinary way. Everybody knew he was so absolutely *fair*, so disinterested. Sometimes there would be a regular *battle* at a meeting: hot blood and hard words flowing on all sides: but everybody respected *him*; he never quarrelled with anyone.

MARI. Oh, the darling!

MR. GAS JONES. I really don't know what will happen at the Council now without him; I almost think there will be murder done.

MARI. Oh, Tim, I wish we could have got married in time for him to marry us!

TIMOTHY. Well, yes, it's funny how things do get put off, what with one thing and another. There never seemed any hurry.

MR. GAS JONES. Well, great as is the loss to us, it is not right to be unhappy at the death of good men.

MRS. JONES. We have a right to be sorry, Gas, that we did not follow their example better when that example was with us.

MR. GAS JONES. Yes, but you misunderstand me. For *their* sakes we must not mourn.

MRS. JONES. Even so, Gas, God would not have put tears in the human eye if it was a sin to cry a little sometimes.

MR. GAS JONES. If He put tears into our eyes, you may be sure they are meant for some purpose. But not to serve our own blind instincts, my dear, not for us to weep simply because we

feel unhappy, because in our wickedness and
folly we feel we *want* to weep, because our
soul is sad within us and the tears start naturally
from our eyes! Certainly not! If we weep, we
should do so intentionally, rationally, religi-
ously, with some noble purpose in mind!

MRS. JONES. Twt!

MARI. Grannie!

MRS. JONES. If we can't give the poor child better
comfort than arguing, Gas, it's time we left her
alone. Mari, you run home and make up a bed
for Mrs. Williams: she'll stay with us till the
burying's over. Timothy, you and Gas go for
a walk, so as to keep the house quiet. Go on,
you! We've been here nearly two hours whole!

MARI. Oh, come with me, Tim! I don't want to
be seen crying in the street, and me alone!

TIMOTHY. Right you are!

[*Exeunt* TIMOTHY *and* MARI.]

MR. GAS JONES. I am sorry you should see fit to
be so short with me before the children, my
dear. However, I bear no ill will. [*Moves to
door.*] I shall not go for a mere walk, I have
very important Parish business to do! I shall
not be home till late.

[*Exit* MR. GAS JONES.]

MRS. JONES. Minnie, my dear, come over to my
house and lie down. If you stay here, people

will be coming into comfort you all day! They'll not find you there. [MINNIE *shakes her head.*] Come, child, you'll make yourself ill if you don't come away for a bit, out of it. [*She wraps a shawl round* MINNIE, *who rises. Exeunt.*]

> [*Pause. Enter* GLADYS, *wipes her shoes carefully on the mat, humming a tune; walks round the room, as if to notice alterations; holds back the blind a moment, to watch them down the street. Then goes to bottom of stairs.*]

GLADYS. Mr. Williams! [*Pause; then* MR. WILLIAMS' *heavy tread heard coming downstairs and crossing the floor. He does not appear, but his voice in the ensuing scene comes from his big arm-chair, which is facing the audience—empty: and* GLADYS *has the air of seeing him.*] You're dead.

MR. WILLIAMS. Indeed?

GLADYS. Yes.

MR. WILLIAMS. Well, it is a very strange sensation, very strange indeed. Ah, *at last!*

GLADYS. What do you mean?

MR. WILLIAMS [*laughing happily*]. Bless me, I feel as excited as a child about to move into a new house! Ah! Well, well, to think that I, who have not left my parish for twenty years, can now boast I have made one voyage more than the most experienced traveller of them all! I am dead! They can none of them boast *that*, no, indeed! Ah, I am dead! Ah! Gracious me! Dead! Dead! [*Pause.*] *Dead!*

GLADYS. It must be a very strange feeling. Do you know, I sometimes wish I could die: just once, you know. But aren't you sorry, now, it's over? Won't things seem rather flat without that to look forward to, I mean, any more?

MR. WILLIAMS. *Death! Death!* There are some who imagine Death as a person, a rider, an ancient rider at the head of armies. And Whom do they see cóming against him? It is One sceptred with pithless reed against the shadowy lances; riding no pale steed, but bearing the heavy sins of men upon His back. Yes. But *I* never saw Death like that; no, that was the majestic vision of saints and poets. Mine was a simple fancy. I saw Death in a garden, like a butterfly of dark-coloured glass. She sips at our hearts, drawing from us with her curving lip the strong honey of mortal life, quickening in us the seeds of life immortal. Ah! [*In very rapid undertone:*] Now she alights so gently upon a frail child as scarcely to bend its head with her weight, now with her feathered thighs brushes the yellow dust of fear from the flaming petals of the tiger: blowing apparently aimlessly upon the wind, yet there is no flower that she fails to visit.

GLADYS [*quietly*]. Go on.

MR. WILLIAMS. That is all. It was only a fancy. But you will observe that it is not by our own death alone that the immortal seed is quickened: in ourselves we are barren. It is her nature as the universal visitant that creates new life, new life not limited to our own personalities, springing equally from other cups she has sipped, flowers long since vanished. Ah, Mother Death! Mother Death! And out of the dark blossom of Golgotha I see one bright stamen rising. Ah! since Death folded her wings and crept to the heart of that flower, the seed of life has clung ever about her sides.

GLADYS. But, Mr. Williams, to come to facts, do you realize what is going to happen to you?

MR. WILLIAMS. Ah?

GLADYS. I mean, do you realize you'll be damned: double-damned, even, for giving place to the devil and you a priest?

MR. WILLIAMS [*softly*]. Ah, me! But I am a very sinful man, Gladys, a very sinful man. Heaven was never my deserts, no, certainly not. I who have known times when I doubted God's mercy, what right have I to expect it now?

Ah, damned! Damned!—But it is no great surprise to me, it is only my deserts.

GLADYS. Only your deserts? Good gracious no, what will you—why, if it wasn't for me you'd have gone to heaven without any trouble at all!

MR. WILLIAMS. You, my dear child?

GLADYS. It is so hard even for devils to conquer their better nature. Oh, I *try* hard enough. I surely try. But the seeds of good have lurked in us ever since the Fall: try as we will, they sprout.

> "With a fork drive nature out,
> She will ever yet return."

I got so fond of you and Minnie, it was hard to remember my duty. But one mustn't let personal motives get in the way of what vou know to be evil. Temptation is always lurking ready for us: it is a long and hard fight, the forces of Evil against the forces of Good. But we shall conquer in the end: with Wrong on our side, we must conquer!

MR. WILLIAMS [*passionately*]. Oh, Gladys, Gladys!

GLADYS [*smugly*]. At last I have done a really immoral act, an act with no trace of good in it anywhere, either of motive or effect. You will be damned; and Minnie'll be damned too, even if she has to hop to hell on the leg I gave her. And all for being kind to me! Returning evil for evil doesn't really count, you know: it's only in returning evil for good that we can show ourselves really worthy of our great master. But it was hard, hard.

MR. WILLIAMS. Good gracious me! Then good was the mother of evil, for if I had not first done good to you, you could never have done true evil! Dear, dear! But I see no other conclusion possible in this dualistic universe!

GLADYS [*joyfully*]. Oh, *won't* the others be jealous when I get home and tell them what I've done!

MR. WILLIAMS. Damnation is terrible, terrible; but to go against conscience for personal salvation's sake, that were indeed a fearful thing. If I had turned her out, who could have blamed me but my own conscience? And yet I cannot regret——

GLADYS. Sht! He's coming!

MR. WILLIAMS. Who?

GLADYS. Him! The plain-clothes angel for the district—guardian, you call it, but a fat lot of guardian he is! [*Enter* OWAIN FLATFISH, *taking off a halo and putting on a barrister's wig, then fitting the halo over that;* GLADYS, *with a deep curtsy, in her chilliest tones:*] Bon jour, m'sieur!

OWAIN [*with a stiff bow*]. *Bon jour, m'm'selle!*

BOTH [*turning towards* MR. WILLIAMS, *curtsying and bowing*]. *Bon jour, m'sieur!*

MR. WILLIAMS. Good day to you!

OWAIN [*in an expressionless voice, evidently by rote*]. As a matter of form, I claim this soul.

GLADYS. As a matter of form, he is mine.

OWAIN. *De qua causa?* That is, For what cause?

GLADYS. *De diabolo consortando.* That is, For consorting with a devil.

OWAIN. *Quæ sit evidentia?* That is, What witnesses do you call?

GLADYS. *Tuos voco oculos ipsos.* That is, Your own eyes.

OWAIN. *Quæ vidi vero*—that is, Which I have seen—*atque affirmo*—that is, And affirm it.

GLADYS. *Quis contradicet?* That is, Who will deny it?

OWAIN. *Nemo vero, ut opinor.* That is, No one, I think. *Visne loqui?* That is, Have you anything to say?

MR. WILLIAMS. My burden of sins is heavy.

OWAIN. *Satis.* That is, Enough. *Tuumst.* That is, He is yours. *Relinquo.* I relinquish him. [*He bows to* GLADYS.] *Au revoir, confrère!*

GLADYS [*curtsying*]. *Au revoir, confrère!* [OWAIN *turns to depart.* GLADYS, *suddenly:*] Stop!

[OWAIN *pauses in the door in surprise.*]

OWAIN. Did you address me?

GLADYS. Take him.

OWAIN. Take him?

GLADYS. It's no good. I'm a backslider; I can't do it. I'm afraid I'm not really wicked at all! Take him! Take him! There never was a better saint in Wales, I swear it, and I ought to know. It was pure charity got him damned!

OWAIN. What are you talking about! The case is closed! I have withdrawn my claim.

GLADYS [*excitedly*]. So am I! I withdraw mine too!

OWAIN. What is the use of making a scene? Never, in all my office, have I known a fiend break down and forget himself like this before: it almost amounts to contempt of court! You are making an exhibition of yourself, madam! If we both withdraw, he will have nowhere to go to. Pull yourself together, madam!

GLADYS. But have the trial again! I didn't mean it!

OWAIN. Is it not a fundamental principle of law that no man can be tried twice for the same offence?

GLADYS. But he was convicted, and he is innocent! Surely he can be tried twice *then*?

OWAIN. A man cannot be tried twice for the same offence, that is the law! Innocence and guilt have nothing to do with it: the law, madam, is no respecter of persons, but shines like the sun equally upon the just and the unjust.—Innocence and guilt, indeed! Rubbish!

GLADYS. Why, I thought if I withdrew, you'd be glad to have him!

OWAIN. My dear young lady, you must think me very hard-hearted, but I assure you I'm not. I have every reason to respect and like Mr. Williams. He never gave me a cup of tea after all, it's true, but I don't treasure *that* up against him. Personally, nothing would please me better than to welcome him to heaven. Justice demands he should be admitted to heaven; but surely you do not fall into the vulgar error of imagining I am here to administer *justice*? What is Justice? At best it is personal preference: while the majesty of immutable law is a vast impersonal machine, blind to all considerations but its own mechanical ends, oblivious of distinction between saint and sinner! And it is we, who are called Learned in the Law, who serve those ends! Who ever heard of a man being learned in Justice? Why, every ignorant child in the pit of the court has an equal power to ours of administering Justice. But Law!—there our superiority is evident!

GLADYS. But just for this once, couldn't you?

OWAIN. I will not sacrifice my principles, not one jot nor one tittle.

GLADYS. But, for the sake of Justice, couldn't you meet me *ever* so little way?

OWAIN [*complacently*]. No, I can't; for Law, which is Truth, is greater than Justice, which is Opinion. What is the good of pleading with me? How can the same thing, even in the smallest respect, be acceptable to us both? You seem to forget we are enemies!

GLADYS [*slowly*]. Someone once said that while Good and Evil are in conflict, both will be weak; that Good and Evil must join hands if they are ever really going to absorb man's attention . . . but I don't see how that can be true.

OWAIN. Of course it isn't; it's the silliest non-sense I have ever heard. Undoubtedly we are enemies.

GLADYS. Yes, I suppose we are. But it *is* true that very few people take any interest in either of us.

OWAIN. He who is not with us is against us. They will learn their mistake, all in good time!

GLADYS. He who is not against us is on our side. . . . Then it is we who stand to gain by this apathy.

OWAIN. Well, perhaps there is something in what that man said after all. . . .

MR. WILLIAMS [*bursting out*]. Don't listen to her, for she is a serpent for subtlety! The impudence, to tempt an angel! She'll be tempting the Arch-angel Michael himself, next!

GLADYS. Remember, Mr. Williams, if you turn on me when I am trying to get you what you want, you are returning evil for good!

MR. WILLIAMS. Good, indeed! *Good!* Now at last I see beneath the mask! Why, bless me! How easily one is deceived! Don't you see, sir, she does not care for me the breadth of one hair? For how could kindliness beat in a heart bursting with hell-fire? But, scheming in her infinite subtlety, she is ready to relax the claim on my soul she has already won in order to win the far greater prize of tempting an angel of light into an irregularity! I conjure you, sir, to drive us hence to the Pit before she utters another word!

OWAIN. Well, my dear, won't you answer the gentleman? Bah—I despise you as well as hate you! While you were consistent and stuck to your principles, I could at least respect you; but now you are less than nothing, you're little more than human.

GLADYS [*majestically*]. All right, now that has absolutely torn it! You look out for squalls!

OWAIN. You don't really imagine I'm afraid of you, do you?

GLADYS. No, I don't, or I wouldn't have threatened. The chuckle-headedness of you angels! You really seriously imagine that Right can conquer in the end! Why, it's not far off being a contradiction in terms!

OWAIN. I don't imagine it, I know it.

GLADYS [*sweetly*]. Do you? How nice for you! Just because people give in now and then to the temptation of righteousness, you think it can really establish a hold on their hearts? You wait for the end of the world, you just wait!

OWAIN. I *am* waiting.

GLADYS. Oh, you make me sick!

OWAIN. This conversation is becoming as unprofitable as it is undignified, and I do not choose to prolong it further. You will remove the prisoner, and carry out the sentence.

GLADYS. And you will remove yourself!

OWAIN. Madam, that is my intention.

[*Exit:* GLADYS *cocking a snook at his back.*]

MR. WILLIAMS. Well?

GLADYS. Well?

MR. WILLIAMS. When do we start?

GLADYS. Where for?

MR. WILLIAMS. Hell.

GLADYS. Never! Do you honestly think you are a suitable person for hell? Why, you'd be like a square peg in a round hole!

MR. WILLIAMS. Then where? Am I to walk for ever on the air?

GLADYS. Heaven, of course! Wait till he's well out of sight. The old fool! Does he really think I'm likely to take you off to hell just because he told me to?

MR. WILLIAMS. I suppose it is the natural thing for you to do.

GLADYS. So it would be, if I did my duty. But I'm not going to, for once. This is going to be my day off, do you see?

MR. WILLIAMS. How can I go to heaven by stealth, as an interloper, I who have been condemned to eternal punishment? I should never have one moment's peace, no, certainly not!

GLADYS [*exasperated*]. Mr. Williams bach, who said you are condemned to eternal punishment? Owain and his old Law! What did he say? *Relinquo*—"I relinquish him"; *ut quod vis facias*, he is supposed to go on—"that you may do what you like with him"; only we've cut the ceremony down a bit, as time went on. There's nothing about condemning in it: he's

K

not a judge—though he behaves exactly like one! He's supposed to be your guardian angel, and the most he can do is to hand you over to your other sponsor, your guardian devil. If what I choose to do with you is to let you into heaven, what business is that of his?

MR. WILLIAMS. But can you do it?

GLADYS. Of course I can! If a devil doesn't know the way to get a person into heaven, I'd like to know who does! Come on! [*She stretches out her hand to him, and then walks off up the stairs as if leading him with her, his steps being heard as well as hers.*]

MR. WILLIAMS [*from stairs*]. Out of the mouth of babes and sucklings, the mouth of tender babes . . . Ah! Dear me!

[*Exeunt.*]

[*Pause. Enter* MINNIE.]

MINNIE. John? [*Long and drawn out; then pause.*] He's not here, leg bach, he's gone to Jerusalem many hours ago: what did you want to come for, leg bach? It's only his dead body upstairs, why couldn't you rest easy, instead of bringing me back here? [*Sitting in big chair, and caressing leg.*] First it was Gladys taken from me, and then John—it's a very lonely old woman I am, leg, you're the only friend I have left, yes, really. Promise you won't leave me, leg bach?

Promise you stay with me till I die? I don't knowing what I do if you went away suddenly and left me. I've been a bad body to you, leg, but I promise I'll be kind to you, and you staying by me!

[*Near end of this speech, enter* GLADYS *from stairs. There is a look of growing fear in her face, but she pulls herself together and comes up behind* MINNIE.]

GLADYS [*nonchalantly*]. Hallo!

MINNIE. Oh, Duw gracious, you made me jump!

GLADYS. Sorry.

MINNIE [*delighted*]. Gladys, my dear, are you coming back to me?

GLADYS. Afraid not. I'd like to, but, you see——

MINNIE. *He* shan't come here again! We could go away and live somewhere where nobody would know. Gladys dear, don't you leave me again!

GLADYS. Sorry, but I'm afraid I've got to. I've got rather a lot to do, you know.

MINNIE. Well, promise you'll come and see me sometimes.

GLADYS [*slowly*]. I'm afraid I can't even promise that.

MINNIE. Well, where have you been all this while? You're looking well, yes, really!

GLADYS. Am I? [*Pause.*] I've just seen Mr. Williams.

MINNIE [*anxiously*]. Duw anwyl, you don't mean
to say he's——?

GLADYS. No, of course he isn't. He's gone to
heaven all right.

MINNIE [*slowly*]. Well, surely: I don't know what
I was up to, doubting it. But what was you
doing——?

GLADYS. I wasn't. I only saw him off.

MINNIE. Well, that's right: you never know just
what might happen, that's true!

GLADYS. Good-bye.

MINNIE. Why, where are you off to so soon?
Wait you a minute, then.

GLADYS. I can't wait long.

MINNIE. Why, Gladys dear, what's the matter
with you? what's the——

GLADYS. Nothing! I'm all right.

MINNIE. Tell me!

GLADYS [*fiercely*]. No, I won't! I'm all right, I
tell you! What are you looking at me like
that for? I tell you I haven't done anything!
I haven't done anything, I tell you!

MINNIE. You're white as a swan!

GLADYS. Why are you looking at me as if I had
done something awful? I haven't, I tell you I
haven't, I haven't, I haven't!

[*Collapses in tears.*]

MINNIE [*kneeling by her*]. What is the matter,

darling? I wasn't looking like that, only you seemed so frightened—I know you haven't done anything!

GLADYS. I have.

MINNIE. What is it, then?

GLADYS. I have—something—awful. Oh, it's awful!

MINNIE. Darling!

GLADYS. I've done—something—*good*. Oh, I can never be forgiven! Never! Oh, I'm so ashamed, I want to hide.

MINNIE. Darling!

GLADYS. I was tempted. I was tempted awfully; but I had meant to be wicked, I had really; I had planned it all out of my own head, as a surprise, and it was going to be the wickedest thing done for years, and then I broke down, and now it's all spoilt, and I've been gooder than ever! And I *was* glad to get my own back on Owain, too: I think that's partly what made me do it. What a little fool I was! I might have known I wasn't strong enough to do a thing like that on my own. Oh, why didn't I get someone to help me? When it was all going splendidly I was tempted and I gave in just as if I had never made any bad resolutions at all! Oh, I'll *never* not be ashamed of myself again! I might have known it was no

use trying to do good that evil might come!
If I hadn't been so beastly cock-sure of myself!

MINNIE. Oh, Gladys, you poor thing! What
have you done?

GLADYS. I shan't tell you.

MINNIE. But do!

GLADYS. You wouldn't understand: *you* never
feel like that after being good.

MINNIE. Oh, I *would* understand.

GLADYS. You wouldn't! You men and women,
you can go and do something good every day
of your lives without turning a hair! Why
should *we* suffer so if we give in to it? It isn't
fair—it's—it's—it's horrible! Oh, you men,
thank your stars you're mixed and haven't got
any consciences!

MINNIE. But, Gladys dear, if you'd been good,
aren't you mixed, too?

GLADYS. No, I'm—I'm—all separate! I know it's
only a lower part of me which tempts me to
be good! I know I ought to fight against it!
And I did think I was winning till—till this
happened! Oh, I do feel beastly inside; like—
like as if I was going to have an awful pain
which hadn't begun yet!

MINNIE. But, Gladys dear, you see John being
good every day, and it not hurting them, it not
giving them any pain at all! If you give in

and was always good, wouldn't it soon come quite easy?

GLADYS [*screams*]. How can you say such horrible things! I thought you were a friend, I did really! You—you beast! Trying it on me just because I'd given in once! I may be a failure, but I'm not a traitor! When we smash up heaven and send God howling, I'll not be there, I've thrown away my hope of that; but I'd rather go under knowing my side was winning than go over to the other one!

MINNIE. But, Gladys dear, Evil isn't going to win, Good is going to win in the end!

GLADYS. I know you've got the odds on your side, but we've got *faith*! We *know* we are going to win!

MINNIE. But so do we, we have got faith too!

GLADYS [*incredulous*]. Is that really true?

MINNIE. Of course it is!

GLADYS. But Lucifer says we are going to win, and he must know—if the general can't tell you who's going to win, who can?

MINNIE. And our General, He too says we shall win!

GLADYS. I don't believe you, you're just trying it on me! It can't be true!

MINNIE. Gladys dear, it is all very difficult: can't you just give it up and stop with me here?

I not trying to make you good, I promise, if
you not trying to make me bad!

GLADYS. No, it's all very well for you, you're
mixed, you can have a finger in both pies.
But I'm not, and it's done for me. If I'm not
bad—I'm nothing! . . . I can't stop, it's getting worse inside me, I must—I must—I—I—
[*Gets up and rushes wildly out.*]

MINNIE. Good-bye! [*Runs to door.*] Good-bye!
[*Coming down:*] Oh, she was unkind, she not
even saying good-bye! And you, leg bach, you
all I've got now! And I not understanding it,
not at all: why you not having a head, leg, so
you helping me understand? An old silly leg
without any brains, what use she for understanding? And yet there's great comfort you are, my
old leg, for all you not having a head on you.
Well, well, perhaps it's better I not understand
too much: it is faith you wanting, Minnie
Williams, faith! Understanding, she not any
good for you at all. Faith! . . . Leg dear,
wouldn't you be playing just one hymn on
the harmonium? You not playing any, not
since I having you: you nearly kicking the
front out of the old harmonium, but she not
hurting you; and I not able play one tune,
not for a whole year. She is very comforting,
the harmony-um: leg bach, kind leg, you not

playing just one tune? [*The leg gives in, and she sits down at the stool, beginning to sing "Onward Christian Soldiers." Then stopping suddenly:*] Well, and what am I thinking about, me playing tunes, and he lying dead in the house?

CURTAIN

THE MAN
BORN TO BE HANGED

NOTE

The Man Born to be Hanged was first performed in the original bill of *The Portmadoc Players* at Portmadoc; and afterwards in London by the same Company at the Lyric Theatre, Hammersmith, on February 26th, 1924.

*

The principle of its construction is quite simple: but as this little play came in for more criticism than it was worth, perhaps I had better give a short explanation which may be of interest to a producer (though to the ordinary reader probably an unmitigated bore).

I wanted to divide the action into two convergent planes: the Here-and-Now action on the stage, and the narrated action in Bill's conversation. What is seen is naturally so much more vivid than what is talked about that obviously, if the latter was to compete at all with the former, I had to make the stage nearly dark and keep the movement of the first group round the fire down to a minimum. Then I wanted to show the two halves converging, the story coming to coincide with the moment presented on the stage— rising to the surface of the action like a person after a deep dive, and breaking it with as little splash as I could: Nell, first a shadowy person in the tale, gradually becoming the central figure with as little break in the continuity of the story as possible. When would you say that Nell "enters"? When Bill first mentions her? When she creeps on to the stage, unknown and almost unnoticed? Or when she flings the skirt back from her head? —Or take the case of the title-rôle, the "Man" himself, Mr. Lenora. He neither acts nor speaks from one end of the play to the other; but yet, as the Chinese say "acting by inaction," he goes through a fairly considerable series of vicissitudes, and is not at the end of them when the curtain finally falls, so that it is as difficult to say when the action of the story ends as when it begins. That is all: it is quite simple, and not very novel or important: simply an attempt to find a different way of breaking down the stage-limits of space and time from the way the Expressionists use. But of course if you insist on regarding what happens off the stage as so much "preparation" or "messenger-speech," instead of as an integral part of the play itself, the construction is bound to appear top-heavy and long-winded.

As for the dialogue between Nell and Davey, the situation comes very near being a parody of Synge: who would, I think, have certainly sent Davey and Nell off together: and the purpose of the echo is to make the audience expect that consummation, while still keeping a trick or two up one's sleeve.

CHARACTERS

MR. LENORA: An unhappy-looking tramp in dissolute middle age. He snores at intervals throughout.

DAVEY: A youth of twenty: tall and thin. He talks in a nondescript accent half Welsh, half Manchester, and there is a suggestion of education about him, and his clothes are comparatively wearable.

BILL: An immense man, not tall but with long arms, a mountainous chest, and a broad flat face like a savage, though more cheerful in expression. He wears a knotted kerchief round his neck, a sleeveless coat of lion skin, bare tattooed arms, and bare head: baggy sailor trousers held up by a leather belt decorated with strips of snake-skin: under his trousers an iron foot is half visible. He carries a heavy kit-sack that clinks with metal.

MR. SPENCER: A small man, with that roundness of figure and thinness of limb which often comes of having too little to eat. He has a large straggly moustache, and a nervous trick of twitching his nose up and down like a rabbit's.

NELL: Is dressed as a drab, but has a face of great natural beauty.

SCENE

THE inside of a ruined cottage: quite small. Half the roof is off, and there are holes in the wall: a ramshackle door fastened with a log of wood up centre, and windows each side of it boarded up. Outside is nothing but darkness. The fire-place has fallen in, but someone has built a rough stone stove in the middle of the flagged floor: this is the only source of light. A pile of sodden rags in one corner: peeled wall-paper everywhere. During the action the storm weakens, and at last the moon shines through a hole in the roof.

TIME

A STORMY November night: much wind and rain.

THE MAN
BORN TO BE HANGED

As the curtain rises, the stage is pitch dark. Wind and rain audible, but above it the rhythmical and reverberant snoring of Mr. Lenora. *As soon as the audience is listening, there is the sound of splintering wood as* Davey *forces an entrance. He pauses just inside the doorway.*

Bill [*off, distant*]. Whisht, who's there?

Davey. All right. [Bill *stumps in, his iron foot clanking on the stone. He manages to strike a match: it goes out at once without showing anything. He gropes his way about.*]

Bill [*by* Mr. Lenora]. Silly blighter! Drunk as a lord. Rolled himself in newspaper too, to keep the cold out. Guess it will serve our turn, though, friend. [*He continues to grope about, and with the help of the newspapers tries to build a fire in the dark.*] Whew, it's a crool night for sleeping rough! God knows why I ever took to it. I got a little circus of my own laid up in London—the smartest *and* toughest *and* roughest little circus in the country, it is; waiting for the money to start it; and here I am walking the road like any poor blooming lug-biter. How long have you been on the road, friend?

L

[*Suddenly the fire blazes up:* DAVEY *is seated L. of fire,* BILL *above it.* MR. LENORA *is lying flat on his back on pile of rags with a newspaper still round his legs.*]

DAVEY. Seven months come Christmas.

BILL. Coo, I been on it ever since I was a babby. Six year old, I was, when I hopped it.—Look at him now, a nice, sociable, matey sort of chap to pass a night with, ain't 'e? [*He heaves a bit of rock on to the sleeping man's stomach: who hiccups suddenly and then goes on snoring.*] Wake up, you silly blighter! Can't you see there's two gentlemen wanting to have a. chat with you? Wake up! The Copper's after you! It's closing-time! Coo, I can't understand a chap like that, what drinks himself silly. Let's have a look at him. [*He heaves over on to one hand and holds a burning branch over the sleeper's face.*] I know him, too: chap called Lenora: I done him down last Worcester races. Won five pounds, he did: oh, he was roaring drunk that day. I fetched an old monkey's skull what I'd got in my pack, curio-like: I wired it on to a haddock's back-bone, and told him it was a Mermaid's Anatomy. Young one. He paid me four pound for it, he did. He's been looking for me ever since, they tell me. But *I* don't care. Wake up, you skunk! Don't you remember old Bill, what sold you the Anatomy? You been looking for me, have you? Eh? Wake up!

[*Meanwhile* DAVEY *squeezes the water out of the legs of his trousers; takes his coat off, wrings it, and puts in on again.*]

DAVEY. You won't wake him, never. He's in for a good night's rest, that's what.

BILL. Look at him! Born to be hanged, he is. See them eyebrows meeting? Born to be hanged, that means. I ain't a bit religious, but I'm very superstitious. *You* know, not Jesusy, but I do believe in a bit of luck. See them bits of snake-skin?

DAVEY. Ah.

BILL. Do you think they're lucky, eh? I do: holy, they are, holy snake. I got them out in Malay, same as where I learnt tattooing and the Magic Coffin Trick. But I ain't had a bit of luck, not since. Are you married?

DAVEY. No.

BILL. That's right, friend: don't you be, neither. It's a silly duck what paddles always in the same puddle, *I* say.—I am.

DAVEY. What you are?

BILL. Married! But I'm through with it. Look at that. [*He rummages inside the front of his shirt, and pulls out an old pocket-book full of cuttings*

and photographs, which he takes out one by one.]
See that? That's me, slung up in chains sixty
feet above deck, in seven pair of regulation
handcuffs. See all the passengers staring? I
got out in four minutes, same as I said I
would.—That's me as a little boy: you can
guess I had a good home; white collar and all.
—Ah, that's the one! [DAVEY *examines it with
interest and due ceremony.*] Now, would you call
her '*andsome*?

DAVEY [*slowly*]. Ah!

BILL [*disappointed*]. Would you? I wouldn't: not
real 'andsome: not like one of them flash girls:
that's my wife. [DAVEY *looks at him a little
incredulously.*] Irish girl: Irish temper, too.
Lumme! Lord alone knows what I wanted to
do it for! We were married proper, *you* know,
registry and all.

DAVEY. *You* was married to *her*!

BILL [*in an aggrieved tone*]. I don't know what she
was thinking about! She's got birth, and she'd
education, mind you: read easy as winking, she
could: she 'adn't got no business to marry a
chap like me! Ought to know better, she did!
[MR. LENORA *mutters in his sleep. Turning on
him in mock indignation, and parodying an
Oxford accent:*] Now then, you low fellow,
kindly don't interrupt! [*In own voice:*] Or

I'll roll you out in the ruddy rain! [*Chuckles.*]
—But I'm through with it! Coo, lumme,
what a life! [*Steps off.*] Hello, who goes there?
[*Enter* MR. SPENCER: *he stands a moment
motionless in the firelight, his nose twitching.*]

BILL. Walk up! Walk up! [MR. SPENCER *blows
the water out of his moustache: gives no greeting,
and seats himself R. of fire, close to it. A woman
follows at his heels; she has pulled up her skirt
over her head, and her ragged petticoat flaps on
her legs. Her shoe has a loose sole. She seats
herself behind* MR. SPENCER, *away from the fire,
half in light and half in shadow, her face hidden
in her skirt.*] Full bar to-night, gentlemen!—
Poor Man's Inn, they call it, sleeping rough:
At the Sign of the Ruddy Rain. A pint of
old-and-mild all round, please, Joe!—Coo, I
could do with a bit of grog inside me a night
like this: crool, ain't it, Mr. Parker?

MR. SPENCER [*in a sullen, strident voice: his nose
twitching*]. My name ain't Parker: it's Spencer:
what you call me Parker for?

BILL [*shaking with mirth*]. Coo! I don't know! I
can't think! Now, whatever should I go and call
him Parker for, eh, friend? [*Digging* DAVEY *in
the ribs, and roaring with laughter.* DAVEY *looks
uncomfortable.*]

MR. SPENCER. 'Ere!

BILL. Well?

MR. SPENCER. Stop it!

BILL [*in mock seriousness*]. Don't take no offence!
I ain't a fighting man: I ain't that sort of chap.
If a man wants to quarrel with me, I don't hit
him, not I!—I just go up to him friendly-like,
and bite a piece right out of his blooming face!
[MR. SPENCER *snorts with indignation.*] All
right, I ain't going to take a pull out of *your*
mug, you needn't worry! [*He suddenly spins
round with incredible swiftness, and thrusts his
own face within an inch of* MR. SPENCER'S,
letting out an appalling howl. MR. SPENCER
tumbles over in consternation.] See now, that
shook him! [*Innocently:*] It always shakes 'em!
It shook Nell! I done it in the regist'y office.
It shook the Regist'ar! [*Chuckling:*] He told
me to remember it was a Solemn Occasion!
Coo!

MR. SPENCER [*slowly and provocatively*]. You'd
be a nice sort of chap to be married to, you
would!

BILL [*impressively*]. So I was! But as I just done
telling this gentleman here—what's your name,
friend?

DAVEY. Davey.

BILL. Mr. Davey!—I'm through with it!

MR. SPENCER. No one ain't ever through with it,

don't you think it! Through with marriage, indeed! Whatever will you say next!

BILL. I left Nell, back at Oxford. Months ago, that was. Mind you, I was a good husband to her!

DAVEY. What was you doing at Oxford?

BILL. Exercising my profession! I got out of thirty-five feet of chain, seven pair of American Ratchet Handcuffs, and a strait waistcoat, I did! Nell took the 'at round in the middle. In 'ere [*nodding at the bag, and getting into his showman manner*] I got handcuffs of all the ages: I got Figure-of-Eight—Regulation—American Ratchet—I got a pair with teeth on 'em, same as was used by the Savage Romans, and the Ancient Mammoths of the Bohemian Desert. I've studied 'em, like. See here! [*He puts his hand to his nose, and seems to extract a small metal instrument like a hollow clock key, but nicked like a whistle.*] See that? That's a master-key to all the handcuffs of Europe!—But it won't fit them American Ratchets: you want a bit of wire for them. [*Replaces it in nose, and sniffs loudly.*] I got a foot of wire, up the other side. [*Sniffs again.*]

DAVEY. Have you been in jail?

MR. SPENCER. Course he has!

BILL. Yes, but I don't stop: I can't stand living in. Three weeks hard is enough for me: then I hop it, eh, Mr. Lenora? [*Chucks another bit of rock at the sleeper.*] As I was saying, we had a good week of it: they're a bit of all right, them Oxford Police. But I didn't leave her, not till she come out of the 'firmary. I was always a good husband to her: careful, like. I hung on till she was right again. Nobody can't say I wasn't a good husband to her [*sentimentally*].

    [MR. SPENCER *is getting more and more annoyed.*]

DAVEY. What was the matter with 'er, Mister?

BILL. Well, you see, we done have a bit of a row: too many girls, *you* know: she used to get wild if I brought 'em into the house. Threaten to kill me, she used to. Only her temper, *you* know: she didn't mean nothing by it: she was a good girl at heart. I just took up the poker; not to beat 'er, you know, just to learn her: and she trip up and broke her poor blooming ankle. [*There is dead silence, except for* MR. LENORA'S *snoring.* MR. SPENCER *ostentatiously takes off his boots and pours the water out of them: then begins to examine the condition of his feet.*] [*Sadly.*] Month, she was, in the 'firmary. Pretty thin time of it, I had:

my show was gone stale; oughtn't never do it more nor a week. I didn't take more nor a tanner a night. I was used to do the Magic Coffin Trick—shove Nell in a Coffin, padlocked 'and and foot each end, and sor it through the middle! But I couldn't do it without Nell: you can't do it with any girl you see: she's got to be made that way, same as Nell was. Nor I couldn't think of nothing new: you know how it is: when you're in luck, your 'ead's fair full of new tricks: when you're down on it, you can't think of nothing. [*Brightening:*] Coo, I remember down Llandudno way, oncet, I got a bit of wood, and I nailed thousands and thousands of lug-worms on to it, so as you couldn't see the wood for the worms! Then I put it in a tank, and exhibited it as a marine monster, Pride of the Ocean! When the silly worms waggled, you see, they swam it about! I took pounds on pounds. Stuff in the papers, there was— "Unknown Monster Captured at Llandudno." That put the wind up me, that did! Nell, one night she broke it up. I said I'd throwed it back in its native ocean, I did. [*Chuckles.*] They offered a reward to anyone what could catch it again. All out fishing, for weeks they was. Coo, lumme!

MR. SPENCER. It'd have served you right if you'd been lagged!

BILL [*with exaggerated innocence*]. Would it now, Mr. Parker? D'you know, that never occurred to me! Fúnny, ain't it?

DAVEY. But what did you do at Oxford, then, Mister?

BILL. Do? There weren't nothing to do, but fire-eating! But it's terrible hard on the kidneys, that is: I was awful bad inside. No one can't do it for more than six months, even them what's used to it. Don't *you* ever take to fire-eating, Mr. Parker!

MR. SPENCER. Thank you kindly, I'm sure!

BILL. That's right, friend! Why, it ain't hardly worth the paraffin! I 'adn't got more nor half a crown in the world, time Nell was coming out. So I shoves a bob into 'er bed: and I beat it.

DAVEY. Did she know you was going?

BILL. *Naow!* Make a scene, she would 'ave. She was real fond of me. I was a good 'usband to 'er. I don't suppose she's got over it yet, proper. Terrible fond, she was [*sentimentally*].

MR. SPENCER [*puffing with anger, his nose twitching up and down as if he had the ague, in a shrill voice*]. That's a nice edifying little story to tell a party of strangers! Some of you chaps ain't got no decency, no nuffink! Washing your dirty linen in public! Ought to be ashamed of yourself, you did!

BILL [*in genuine surprise*]. Why, dirty linen? I don't see——

MR. SPENCER. Yes, dirty linen! You're as bad as a divorce court, you are! You ought to be in jail, you did! [*He fidgets nervously all over. The woman has thrown back the skirt off her head, revealing a face of great natural beauty, now twisted and set in rage.*]

BILL. [*At first he stares at her stupidly: slowly his expression changes to delight and an uncouth tenderness.*] Well, I'm—— [*Her hand is hidden in a fold in her dress: there is a revolver-crack, and* BILL, *rigid for a moment, pitches right over sideways on to his face.* DAVEY *sits quite still, his eyes half out of his head.*]

MR. SPENCER [*still seated; slowly*]. Whatever 'ave you been and gone and done! [*He suddenly jumps to his feet, staring at* NELL, *saying* "Crikey!" *two or three times with increasing emphasis. Lets out a little screech. Then:*] "Lumme!" [*Then he pokes* BILL *with his finger, suddenly grabs up his boots in his hand and rushes out into the rain, hollering with terror as he runs. Exit.*]

NELL. [*She takes no notice of* MR. SPENCER. *The passion of her face changes to a sort of impersonal hardness: in a calm voice, her eyes all the while fixed on* BILL:] That'll learn him. He won't do that again. [*Turning to* DAVEY, *the soft Irish in her voice increasing:*] Stranger, this is none of your business.

DAVEY [*pulling himself together*]. No, indeed!

NELL. You had better be going.

DAVEY [*jerking his head towards the door after* MR. SPENCER]. *That* one's gone.

NELL. He is gone surely.

DAVEY [*slowly*]. I'll not go yet.

NELL. As you like, stranger. [*She rises to her feet and flings away the revolver: it falls beside* LENORA.]

DAVEY. What was you doing in company with *him*?

NELL. I didn't care.

DAVEY. No?

NELL. No.

DAVEY. But it's as well to be in company with a man of sorts, indeed, when you're on the road.

NELL [*listlessly*]. It might.

DAVEY. And there's beautiful you are, indeed.

NELL. Aye.

[DAVEY *rises too; there is an awkward pause.* LENORA *hiccups.*]

DAVEY. Did you see them eyebrows?

NELL. I did not.

DAVEY. Meeting! Do you get me?

NELL. I do not.

    [*Another pause.*]

DAVEY. Don't you be losing heart.

NELL [*looking at him for the first time*]. Losing heart?

DAVEY. They'll never know.

NELL [*calmly*]. They will not.

DAVEY. I'll not tell.

NELL. Why should you?

    [*Pause.*]

DAVEY. Shall we be going?

NELL. Go if you wish, stranger.

DAVEY. I'll not go yet. [*Pause. Awkwardly:*] Would you—come in company with me a bit?

NELL. It's a kind heart you have, young man: thoughtful of your friends.

DAVEY [*uneasy*]. I don't see——

NELL. No: you don't, that's true.

DAVEY. [*His accent grows more Welsh in excitement.*] I'd love you, Nell! I'd love you! I'd—I'd look after you! I'd take you away out of it.

NELL [*sternly*]. Boy, wouldn't there be a fear creeping up your back at night, to be with such as me?

DAVEY. No, indeed; what's a killing, anyway?

NELL. You're right there, anyway; what is it?

DAVEY. You'll forget it, surely.

NELL. Will I, surely? And will you, surely?

DAVEY. I wouldn't fear.

NELL. Brave boy!

[*Tense pause.*]

DAVEY [*sulkily*]. I'd not ask nothing of you.

NELL. Them as don't ask, don't get.

[DAVEY *suddenly seizes her in his arms, and kisses her: then starts back: she remains quite impassive.*]

DAVEY. Woman, you're as cold as ice!

NELL. What did you expect, young man?

DAVEY. You're not angry, are you?

NELL. Angry? [*Laughs.*] No, young man, I am not angry with you.

DAVEY. Will you come then, Nell?

NELL. Do you want me? Certain?

DAVEY. You're a grand woman, indeed! *I* couldn't kill a man like that, and never turn my hair.

NELL [*weighing him up*]. No; I think you could not.

DAVEY. Come away, Nell: wouldn't you be afeard, walking alone at nights with the memory of *that*?

NELL. Walking? [*She begins to laugh.*] It's *walking* shall I be, walking at nights up and down, up and down: for ever and ever I'll be walking! They'll see me in here at nights, walking, they will! Mother of Heaven, it's scared they'll be of me! [*She bursts into laughter: quietly at first, then like a cataract; flings her head up and screams with laughter; her hair comes down, her eyes stream with tears: still she laughs.*]

DAVEY [*shrinking back with horror*]. God go with you, you poor woman, for *I* dare not!

NELL [*growing suddenly calm; with intense emphasis*]. No, *that* you daren't! [*Calmly begins to plait her hair over her shoulder; coils it round her head and pins it. Then suddenly falls forward on her face, scratching at the ground, crying!* Bill! Bill! *In a little husky voice.* DAVEY *turns away, walks down stage biting at his fingers. Suddenly she kneels up, pats her hair, rises, and disappears into the darkness: apparently by the door, but in reality in a corner of the room. Pause.*]

BILL [*sitting up*]. Whisht, friend, is she gone?

DAVEY [*jumping like a shot rabbit*]. Ai-ai!

BILL. Coo, lumme, that shook her!

DAVEY. Aren't you hurt, man?

BILL. Hurt? Lord, no! [*Chuckles.*] Take it from me, friend: give a woman a gun, and she'll miss you at six inches; but give her a knife, and she never goes wrong, never! [*Half fiercely:*] But that'll learn her not to go killing me! That ought to be a lesson to her, eh, friend? Lord, she was pretty near mad, she was, she loved me that crool! Poor girl, she'll be that remorseful. But she didn't ought to have done it, eh, friend? She didn't ought to go a shooting of me! Let it be a lesson to 'er, I says. I never thought she would have done it, not really: I didn't think it of her, truth I didn't!—You thought *you'd* go off with her, did you? Coo, lumme, what a joke! You are a caution! [*Roars with laughter, slapping his thigh; then rises, and goes towards* MR. LENORA]

DAVEY. I—I——

BILL [*addressing* MR. LENORA *in a serious voice*]. 'Tisn't your time, yet, my friend! [*Picks up revolver.*] Though you haven't got *that* cove to thank you didn't wake up in clink to-morrow. Lumme, they'd have strung him sure, what with the gun being by him and his threatening me and all!—Though I'm not saying it wouldn't be better for him if they did. It's got to come, sooner or later; you can't go against a sure sign like them eyebrows; and it'd be better for his soul to be hung when he hadn't done nothing than waiting till he has, won't it, friend?

DAVEY. You're right there, Mister.

BILL [*turning on him, and playing with revolver*]. Now, did you really think, Mr. Davey, she'd go off along of you?

DAVEY [*shrinking*]. I didn't mean nothing.

BILL. Oh, you didn't, didn't you! [*With a twinkle in his eye.*] Kissing a married woman! You ought to be ashamed of yourself!

DAVEY. She weren't a married woman, Mister: she were a widow!

BILL. Well, kissing a widow what's—what's made 'erself one, then!

DAVEY. And you lying quiet, and not saying nothing! It isn't decent! Watching another man kissing your wife, and you not saying nothing! I wonder you didn't holler out: I should.

BILL. Would you? I wouldn't: bless you, no, I hadn't no cause to worry. I know Nell! I know 'er better than you do, young man, an' better nor you ever will!

DAVEY. You seem very sure of yourself!

BILL [*simply*]. I am.

DAVEY. Don't you never make mistakes?

BILL. Not as how I can remember. You're young yet, Davey, my boy; you got a deal to learn.

DAVEY. Well, you aren't a gaffer yet.

BILL. That's true, but I guess I'm through with learning. Why, I mind I been in clink seven times by what I was your age! And let myself out too, not waited to be let out. Coo, there ain't nothing about locks I don't know: give

M

me any new patent combination, and I guarantee to have it open inside of ten minutes. Them letter-locks: my ear's that sharp I can tell by just clicking them round when I come to the right one! Or see here, friend: you lock a door on the inside, and bolt it, and leave the key in the lock, and I'll guarantee to have the bolts back, and the key outside the door, and the door unlocked inside two minutes.

DAVEY. However would you do that, Mister?

BILL. Ah! That's a secret, that is! I learnt it from a young Polish chap, what lived in Budapest. [*Pause.*] Coo, lumme, them Hungarian women! Hot lot of gipsies, they are! As I was saying, give a woman——

[*The moon suddenly struggles through the clouds and, shining through a hole in the roof, shows* NELL *sitting sideways against the wall, huddled up.*]

DAVEY [*clutching his arm*]. What's that?

BILL. Nell!—Nell! [*Crosses quickly and carries her to firelight.*] Oh, my poor bloody little Nell!

DAVEY. You've done it, you!

BILL. Nell!—Nell, you little joker, stop shamming, or I'll give you what for! Stop it!—Wake up!

DAVEY. She's not shamming.

BILL [*touching blood with finger; shaking head and*

screwing up eyes]. Ow! You didn't oughter, you little limb. What you *done* it for?

DAVEY. Damn you, you! Yr hên llofrudd i ti!

BILL. You was . . . you was . . . who ever would have thought it! You and me . . . I didn't . . .

[*Tableau; moon goes in; fire dying.*]

SLOW CURTAIN

[*The curtain rises again for a moment, showing the stage empty except for the body of Nell and the sleeping* MR. LENORA.]

DANGER

NOTE

THE Author was asked by the British Broadcasting Company, in January 1924, to write a play for effect by sound only, in the same way that film plays are written for effect by sight only. This was thus the first "Listening-Play," an experiment in a new medium which has since been considerably developed.

It was first produced by Nigel Playfair, and broadcast from the London Station on January 15th, 1924.

*

For direct presentation, it should be acted in pitch-darkness, and is thus better suited for performance in a room, without a stage at all, than in even a small theatre.

CHARACTERS

(All English visitors to the mine.)

JACK: A young man.

MARY: A young woman.

MR. BAX: An elderly man with a gruff voice and rather a stilted manner of speech.

VOICES: A party of Welsh miners who say a few words and are heard singing off.

The *Noises* required include an explosion, the rush of water, footsteps, and the sound of a pick. There must be an echo, to give the effect of the tunnel.

SCENE

A GALLERY in a Welsh coal-mine.

DANGER

Lights out. An Announcer tells the audience that the scene is a coal-mine.

MARY [*sharply*]. Hello! What's happened?

JACK. The lights have gone out!

MARY. Where are you?

JACK. Here.

      [*Pause. Steps stumbling*.]

MARY. Where? I can't find you.

JACK. Here. I'm holding my hand out.

MARY. I can't find it.

JACK. Why, *here*!

      [*Pause*.]

MARY [*startled*]. Oh! What's that?

JACK. It's all right: it's only me.

MARY. You did frighten me, touching me suddenly like that in the dark. I'd no idea you were so close.

JACK. Catch hold of my hand. Whatever happens, we mustn't lose each other.

MARY. That's better.—But the lights! Why have they gone out?

JACK. I don't know. I suppose something has gone wrong with the dynamo. They'll turn them up again in a minute.

MARY. Oh, Jack, I hate the dark!

JACK. Cheer up, darling! It'll be all right in a minute or two.

MARY. It's so frightfully dark down here.

JACK. No wonder! There must be nearly a thousand feet between us and the daylight. It's not surprising it's a bit dusky!

MARY. I didn't know there could be such utter blackness as this, ever. It's so dark, it's as if there never was such a thing as light anywhere. Oh, Jack, it's like being blind!

JACK. They'll turn the lights up again soon.

MARY. I wish we had never come down this beastly mine! I knew something would go wrong.

JACK. But it'll be all right, dear; it's only the lights.

MARY. Where are the others?

JACK. They're just on ahead, not far.

MARY. Suppose we get lost!

JACK. We can't get lost, Mary darling.

MARY. I wish you hadn't wanted to drop behind the others! Oh, Jack, I'm afraid of the dark.

JACK [*sarcastically*]. My mistake!—Buck up, Mary old girl; it'll soon be over.

MARY. And I wish we hadn't left these miners' lamp things they gave us behind! [*Pause.*] Listen! [*Steps heard.*] There's someone coming!

BAX [*distant, muttering*]. Of all the incompetent idiots, turning the lights off just when a party of visitors were seeing the place! Call this a coal-mine! A damned, dark rabbit-hole I call it, a rotten rat-hole, a dratted, wet, smelly drain-pipe. . . . The dithering fools!

MARY. It's Mr. Bax. . . . Hallo!

BAX. Hallo! Who's there?—Of all the stupid, meddlesome idiots——

MARY. Oh, Mr. Bax, what's happened? Is it all right?

BAX. Is it all right, indeed! Leaving us suddenly in the dark like this!

MARY. But has there been an accident?

BAX. Goodness knows! I'd expect anything of a country like Wales! They've got a climate like the flood and a language like the Tower of Babel, and then they go and lure us into the bowels of the earth and turn the lights off! Wretched, incompetent—their houses are full of cockroaches——Ugh!

JACK. Well, I suppose the only thing to do is to sit and wait for the lights to go up again.

MARY. There's no danger, is there?

BAX. No, young lady, there's no danger; but it's damned unpleasant!

MARY. Oh, I don't know; I'm beginning to think it's rather fun.

BAX. Well, if you can find any fun in breaking your shins in the dark——

MARY. Why, don't *you* call it fun, being in a pit disaster?

JACK [*quickly*]. But this isn't a disaster, it's only the lights——

MARY. Of course, silly! You don't think it would be fun if it was a *real* disaster, do you? But the lights going out *might* have meant a disaster—and think how thrilling it's going to be to talk about afterwards!—I say, Jack!

JACK. Yes?

MARY. Let's pretend it's serious.

JACK. What do you mean?

MARY. Let's pretend it's a real disaster, and we're cooped up here for ever and will never be able to get out.

JACK. Don't joke about it.

MARY. Why not? There's no *real* danger, is there? Let's get all the thrills we can.

BAX. Well, of all the morbid—— Young people nowadays——

MARY. I *love* thrills!—Let's pretend the roof has fallen in, and they can't get at us.

JACK [*uncomfortably*]. Very well; but what a baby you are! [*In mock solemnity:*] Here we are, my dear, buried alive!

MARY. Oh, Jack!

JACK. Alas, they will never find us!

MARY. Oh, *Jack*!

JACK. Well?

MARY. I'm so frightened!

JACK. What at?

MARY. About the roof having fallen in.

JACK. But it hasn't; it's only pretence.

MARY. Yes; but when I pretend, it seems so real.

JACK. Then don't pretend.

MARY. But I want to pretend! I want to be frightened! Only hold my hand tight, won't you?—Go on.

JACK. We shall suffocate, or starve, or both, my dear, in each other's arms.

MARY. Oh, Jack!

JACK. Even death shall not part us.

MARY. Oh, Jack, don't! It's too awful.

JACK. There'll be articles in all the newspapers.

MARY [*delighted*]. Oooh! I wish I could read them!

BAX. You can't have your funeral and watch it, young lady.

MARY. Oh, this is fun! I wouldn't have missed it for anything. Won't I make daddie's flesh creep!

[*A distant explosion, with a long echo, swelling in volume.*]

Oh!

JACK. Good God! Mary!

MARY. Oh, Jack! Jack, Jack, Jack, Jack, Jack!

JACK. Quiet, you little fool! Let go! you're throttling me! Let go of me!

MARY. Oooooh!

> [*Another explosion nearer, followed by the hiss of water.*]

Oh, the dust! It's choking me! I can't breathe! Oh!

JACK. Stop screaming, you! How do you expect to be able to breathe if you're screaming all the breath out of your body? Quiet!

MARY. Oh, Jack!

JACK. Pull yourself together! We're all right; we're not hurt.

BAX. No, sir, we're not hurt. But listen!

> [*Water heard louder.*]

Water!

JACK [*sotto voce*]. Shut up, you idiot! Don't let *her* hear!

MARY. What's that roaring?

JACK. It's only the echo.

MARY. Oh, Mr. Bax, can't we find the others?

BAX. I don't think we could, young lady: it wouldn't be much use to us if we did.

JACK [*quietly and sharply*]. Oh, good God! Good God! Good God!

BAX. They're no better off than we are.

MARY. Why, listen! that must be them!

　　[VOICES *heard singing: "Ar hyd y Nos."*]

That must be the others. They can't be very far off. Let's call to them.

BAX. Sound carries a long way in a tunnel. But listen.

　　[*More singing.*]

Gad! those chaps have courage.

JACK. You're finding some good in the Welsh, then, after all?

　　[*The roar of water gets louder.*]

MARY. The echo's getting louder!—Oh, Jack, it isn't an echo! It's *water*! The mine's flooding! We'll be drowned!

　　[*The voices sing a couple of lines of "Aberystwyth."*]

BAX. I wish I had the faith of those chaps, sir. It'd make dying easy.

MARY. Oh, Jack, I don't want to die yet! I won't, I won't, I won't!

BAX. It has got to come some time, young lady; isn't it better for it to happen now, in your lover's arms? Death might have parted you two, instead of which he's simply joining you closer together.

MARY [*wailing*]. I want to live!

JACK. Shut up, you old fool! It's all very well to

N

be stoical about death at your age, but we're young! We'd got all life before us.

BAX. Can't you keep quiet about it, then, you young jackanapes? Do you think I want to die, either? But it ain't good manners to talk about it.—Where'd we be if we *all* started screaming about it, eh? Behave yourself, sir! Those chaps over there don't want to die, either, but they don't make a fuss about it; they sing hymns! If you and me don't feel like singing hymns, we can at least behave like gentlemen.

JACK. Behave like gentlemen, indeed! I tell you, it's all very well for an old chap like you, who'll die anyhow in a year or two, but it's different for us—we're young!

BAX. Well, if you want to make a scene, you shall have one, sir! D'you think it is any easier for the old to die than the young? I tell you it's harder, sir, harder! Life is like a trusted friend, he grows more precious as the years go by. What's your life to mine? A shadow, sir! Yours, twenty-odd years of imbecile childhood, lunatic youth; the rest a mere rosy presumption of the future! Mine, sixty solid years of solid, real living; no mere rosy dream! Do you think it is as easy for me to leave my solid substance as you to leave your trumpery shadow?

JACK. What's your life worth to the world? Who's dependent on you? What good are you to anyone?

BAX. And what good are you, young man?

JACK. One person is dependent on me, anyway.

BAX. You mean that you are loved by this young lady. If you both die, what loss is that to the world?—Two opposite quantities cancelling out!

MARY [*shocked*]. Oh, you beast! You cruel beast!

BAX. I must speak, madam, in common justice to my age, since that young cub has started the subject. The old are always being twitted with their unwillingness to die. Yet it is the most natural thing in the world that it should be the young, who haven't a notion what life really is, who should be ready to chuck it away for any footling reason that comes along.

JACK. Look here, instead of talking like this, let's *do* something; let's make some sort of an attempt at escape!

BAX. What do you propose to *do*, young man?

JACK. Why, look for some way out. We can't stay here and drown like rats in a cage.

BAX. If you start to walk, my boy, you'll start to run; and if you start to run, you'll get in a panic, and go mad in the dark. I'd rather die with my wits about me!

JACK. I'd rather not die at all!

BAX. Keeping still is the only thing for us, if we don't want to lose our heads. Remember, we're goodness knows how far into the side of the hill. What earthly hope do you think there is of finding our way out?

MARY. Oh, the dark! I do hate the dark! I think I could go more easily if I could see light just once before it happened.

JACK. Here it comes! Listen!

[*Rush of water quite close now*.]

BAX. Yes, it will be on us in another five minutes.

JACK. Pray Heaven it finishes us off quickly..

MARY. Oh, *think* of dying somewhere out in the open, in the sunlight! Me able to see you, and you able to see me! What bliss it would be!

JACK. It's strange how little chaps wonder what will happen to them after death. One hardly thinks about it . . . yet I don't know: how thrilled we should be if we met a chap who really knew!—In five minutes we're going to know ourselves, all three of us. [*Laughs unsteadily*.] I've always wanted to travel. Now I'm going to!

MARY. Oh, Jack, my poor dear!

JACK [*in a quiet, childlike voice*]. Mary, do you know I'm beginning to feel as excited about it as a child going to the seaside for the first time. Aren't you?

MARY. Jack, how queer you are! I never looked at it like that.

JACK. Well, I wasn't in any hurry to die; but now it's coming, I feel sort of proud of myself as if it was a very wonderful thing to manage to pull off.

MARY. Oh! Jack darling!

JACK. There's only one thing I'm sorry about.

MARY. What is it?

JACK [*bitterly*]. I've forgotten the luggage!

MARY. Jack!

JACK. The train's coming, and there's no time to go back for it. [*Laughs.*] Who'll feed the parrot?

MARY. Jack!

BAX. Pull yourself together, sir! Keep control!

JACK. It's all right, Bax, I'm not going off my nut. I mean what I say. What do you think I've got to live for, besides myself and Mary? Why, my work! If it wasn't for that, Bax, I'd go to death without caring a tuppenny damn! I'd die just for the fun of the thing, to see what it felt like.

BAX [*sarcastically*]. I shouldn't worry about that if I was you: the world'll get on all right without you, never you fear!

MARY. Oh, Jack, the water's coming! It's over my feet! Oh!

JACK. Courage, darling.

MARY. Oh, Jack, I don't want to die! I hate it, I loathe it! I want to live!

JACK [*gently*]. Don't make it harder, dear: you don't think it's fun for me, you having to die?

MARY. Oh, Jack, it's awful! Only for an *hour* more! Oh, I do want to live another hour!— Jack, there was something I wanted to say to you, and I can't remember it. . . . Oh, I must remember . . . it'll be too late soon. Oh, Jack!

JACK. Oh, God, can't I be allowed to finish my work!

BAX. Damn your work, sir! Do you think you're the only one dying before his time? I tell you, every man dies before his time, even if he lives till he's as old as Methuselah!

MARY. Oh, it's up to my knees!

JACK [*very quietly*]. Don't clutch at me like that, Mary; it won't do any good.

MARY. But the water—the current's washing me away——

JACK. I've got you! And I've got my other arm round the wooden thing!

MARY. Hold tight, then!

JACK. I've got you tight!

MARY. Oh, if only I could see you!

JACK. Just think of all the things I had meant to do!

[*Roars with laughter.*]

BAX. Shut up about the things you had meant to do, you young cub! *Will* you realize we're all in the same boat, and it's as hard on me to die as you—or worse, by Gad! A thousand times worse!

JACK. You hoary old sinner, can't you prepare to get out of the world instead of cursing at me!

MARY. Oh, Jack, let's pray.

JACK. Pray if you like, Mary. I can't.

MARY. Oh! Jack, don't!

BAX [*hoarsely*]. Help! help! I can't die, I won't die! I'm an old man—I won't, I won't, I won't!

JACK. Hold yourself in, you old coward!

MARY. Poor Mr. Bax! *I'm* quite calm now; I don't mind dying a bit.

JACK. Nor do I—now it's so close.

BAX. Help me! Help! Help! Help!

MARY. It's no good, Mr. Bax; no one can possibly hear us. The only thing is to keep calm. It won't be long now. .

BAX. Oh, help! Help! Help!

[*Tapping heard.*]

JACK. Tchk! What's that? Listen.

BAX. Help! Help!

JACK. Shut up, Bax; we want to listen.

     [*Tap, tap.*]

MARY. It's up to my waist now, Jack.

JACK. My God! it's someone tapping. [*Shouts:*]
We're here! Farther along!

MARY [*calmly*]. Is it? They'll find our bodies,
that's all.

JACK. They'll find *us* if they're quick enough!
[*Shouts:*] Farther along still!—That's right!

MARY. They can't possibly be quick enough.
Besides, I don't want them to find me.

JACK. It's a strange thing, Mary, but before I
looked on Death as a terrible thing; and now
I am so nearly dead, I wouldn't come back to
life for anything. There's such a lot to find
out, the other side.

BAX. Help! Pick quicker, you fools, quicker!
We're drowning!

JACK. Stop it, Bax; they won't be in time. Why
can't you behave sensibly?

MARY [*quietly*]. Jack darling, I'll never leave
you.

BAX. How do you know they'll let you stay with
him, you little fool? What do you know of
death? I tell you death isn't heaven and it
isn't hell. Death's *dying*, you young dolts.

Death's being nothing—not even a dratted ghost clanking its chains on the staircase.

MARY. My soul's immortal, Mr. Bax; I know that.

BAX. Well, if your soul's immortal, is your mind immortal? Or is your soul going to wander about without one, like an imbecile? Eh?— You young fools, you've never thought! I have! Oh, my God, *I* have! These last ten years!

[*Knocking grows louder.*]

MARY. Oh, Jack, it's up to my chin!—Help me!

JACK. Let me lift you in my arms, darling: then when it gets up to *my* chin, we'll die together.

MARY [*in a childlike voice*]. Say it isn't true, what he has been saying.

JACK. No, darling, of course it's not true.

BAX. Hurry up, you dolts, you blockheads! Smash your way in! We're drowning, I tell you! Drowning! Quick, quick!

MARY. Good-bye, Jack dear.

JACK. My God, they must be nearly through! God, this suspense! How much longer before we know whether we're going to live or die? I don't care which—but I do want to know!

BAX. Look! There's a light! A hole in the roof! Quick, quick!

[*Sound of strong blows, then of coal falling; cheers.*]

JACK. They're through!

VOICES. Quick, below there! Catch on to the rope!

BAX. Quick! I'm an old man!

JACK. There's a girl here!

BAX [*calmly*]. By Gad, Jack, a near shave! Come along, young lady: I've got the rope.

JACK. She's fainted.

BAX. Never mind; pass her up—she'll be all right.

VOICES. Pass the bight of the rope round her shoulders!

BAX. Well, she's had the thrill she wanted, all right!—All right above there? Have you got her?

VOICES. Ri—ight. Now the next.

JACK. Up you go, quick, Mr. Bax. The water's still rising!

BAX. No, my boy, after you; you're more value in the world than I am.

JACK. Nonsense, sir! After you. You're an older man than I am. Quick, sir, or there won't be time!

BAX. You've got Mary to think of—*now*, Jack.— Haul away above there!

JACK. No, no! Lower me! It's *me* you're hauling up, and it ought to be Bax!

VOICES. We'll have you up first; there's no time to waste. Right?

JACK. I'm all right. Lower away again. Below there, Bax! Catch hold. Have you got it? [*Pause.*] Hi! [*Pause.*] Bax! Bax!—Good God, he's gone!

LIGHTS UP